LEMON LAWS

by
Margaret C. Jasper

I.C.C. LIBRARY

Oceana's Legal Almanac Series:
Law for the Layperson

2005
Oceana Publications
A Division of Oxford University Press, Inc.

Information contained in this work has been obtained by Oceana Publications from sources believed to be reliable. However, neither the Publisher nor its authors guarantee the accuracy or completeness of any information published herein, and neither the Publisher nor its authors shall be responsible for any errors, omissions or damages arising from the use of this information. This work is published with the understanding that the Publisher and its authors are supplying information, but are not attempting to render legal or other professional services. If such services are required, the assistance of an appropriate professional should be sought.

You may order this or any Oceana publication by visiting Oceana's website at http://www.oceanalaw.com

Library of Congress Control Number: 2005934571

ISBN 0-379-11420-8

Oceana's Legal Almanac Series: Law for the Layperson
ISSN 1075-7376

To My Husband Chris

Your love and support
are my motivation and inspiration

-and-

In memory of my son, Jimmy

Table of Contents

CHAPTER 3:
YOUR REMEDIES UNDER STATE LEMON LAWS

ABOUT THE AUTHOR

MARGARET C. JASPER is an attorney engaged in the general practice of law in South Salem, New York, concentrating in the areas of personal injury and entertainment law. Ms. Jasper holds a Juris Doctor degree from Pace University School of Law, White Plains, New York, is a member of the New York and Connecticut bars, and is certified to practice before the United States District Courts for the Southern and Eastern Districts of New York, the United States Court of Appeals for the Second Circuit, and the United States Supreme Court.

Ms. Jasper has been appointed to the panel of arbitrators of the American Arbitration Association and the law guardian panel for the Family Court of the State of New York, is a member of the Association of Trial Lawyers of America, and is a New York State licensed real estate broker and member of the Westchester County Board of Realtors, operating as Jasper Real Estate, in South Salem, New York. Margaret Jasper maintains a website at http://www.JasperLawOffice.com.

Ms. Jasper is the author and general editor of the following legal almanacs: AIDS Law; The Americans with Disabilities Act; Animal Rights Law; The Law of Attachment and Garnishment; Bankruptcy Law for the Individual Debtor; Individual Bankruptcy and Restructuring; Banks and their Customers; Buying and Selling Your Home; The Law of Buying and Selling; The Law of Capital Punishment; The Law of Child Custody; Your Rights in a Class Action Suit; Commercial Law; Consumer Rights Law; The Law of Contracts; Co-ops and Condominiums: Your Rights and Obligations As Owner; Copyright Law; Credit Cards and the Law; The Law of Debt Collection; Dictionary of Selected Legal Terms; The Law of Dispute Resolution; Drunk Driving Law; DWI, DUI and the Law; Education Law; Elder Law; Employee Rights in the Workplace; Employment Discrimination Under Title VII; Environmental Law; Estate Planning; Everyday Legal Forms; Executors and Personal Representatives: Rights and Responsibilities; Harassment in the Workplace; Health Care and Your Rights; Hiring Household Help and Contractors: Your Rights and Obligations Under the Law; Home Mortgage Law Primer; Hospital Liability Law; How To Change Your Name; How To Protect Your Challenged Child; Identity Theft and How To Protect Yourself; Insurance Law; The Law of Immigration; International Adoption; Juvenile Justice and Children's Law; Labor Law; Landlord-Tenant Law; The Law of Libel and Slander; Living Together: Practical Legal Issues; Marriage and Divorce; The Law of Medical Malpractice; Motor Vehicle Law; The Law of No-Fault Insurance; Nursing Home Negligence; The Law of Obscenity and Pornography; Patent Law; The Law of Personal Injury; The Law of Premises Liability; Prescription Drugs; Privacy and the Internet: Your Rights and Expectations Under the Law; Probate Law; The Law of Product Liability; Real Estate Law for the Homeowner and Broker; Religion and the Law; Retirement Planning; The Right to Die; Rights of Single Parents; Law for the Small Business Owner; Small Claims Court; Social Security Law; Special Education Law; The Law of Speech and the First Amendment; Teenagers and Substance Abuse; Trademark Law; Victim's Rights Law; The Law of Violence Against Women; Welfare: Your Rights and the Law; What if it Happened to You: Violent Crimes and Victims' Rights; What if the Product Doesn't Work: Warranties & Guarantees; Workers' Compensation Law; and Your Child's Legal Rights: An Overview.

INTRODUCTION

Aside from one's home, an automobile is generally the second largest purchase a consumer makes. Buying an automobile is a very important transaction that must be considered carefully if one does not want to risk a costly mistake. Nothing is more frustrating than spending a large part of your savings for a new car that is in the repair shop more than on the road. This almanac sets forth those items you should consider when purchasing or leasing a new or used car, in order to reduce the likelihood that you will be stuck with a chronically defective car—known as a "lemon."

If you are unlucky enough to be stuck with a lemon car, you should be aware of your rights under state and federal laws, including your right to a replacement car or a refund. All 50 states and the District of Columbia have enacted some type of state lemon law. These laws are based on the federal Magnuson-Moss Warranty Act, which makes breach of warranty a violation of federal law.

This almanac will help you determine if your car is considered a lemon under your state's lemon law. For example, you need to know the criteria your state has developed for deciding whether a car is a lemon. This almanac also sets forth the steps you must take to obtain a replacement car or refund, including the requirements for giving notice to the manufacturer, and how to maintain a proper repair log to support your claim. The lemon law arbitration process is also discussed, including the types of proof you need to support your claim. In addition, the remedies available to you if your car is determined to be a lemon are also explored, including calculating the amount of refund you are entitled to receive.

The Appendix provides applicable statutes, sample forms, and other pertinent information and data. The Glossary contains definitions of many of the terms used throughout the almanac.

CHAPTER 1:
WHAT DO YOU DO IF YOU BOUGHT
A LEMON?

WHAT IS A LEMON?

A "lemon" is a term used to describe a car with a chronic defect that substantially impairs the car's use, value or safety. The key term is "substantial impairment." If the paint has started to peel prematurely, or the radio volume control doesn't work properly, your car will not qualify as a "lemon." However, if the brakes continually fail, or the car doesn't steer properly, after you have tried to have the problem repaired, you likely bought a lemon.

If you think your car is a lemon, you need to know your rights and responsibilities under the law. For example, you need to know the criteria your state has established to determine whether a car is a lemon. In addition, you need to know how to maintain a repair log to support your lemon law claim, and the procedure to follow in order to notify the manufacturer of the defect and obtain a replacement car or refund. This almanac provides the information you need to pursue your lemon law claim.

WHAT IS A LEMON LAW?

All 50 states and the District of Columbia have enacted laws that protect consumers who have purchased a car that turns out to be a "lemon." A lemon law generally entitles the consumers to a replacement vehicle or a refund for a chronically defective car that the manufacturer has been unable to fix despite a reasonable number of repair attempts.

Lemon laws do not cover defects that result from an accident, neglect, or abuse. In addition, there is no coverage for defects that arise from modification or alteration of the car by persons other than the manufacturer or its authorized service agent.

Many state lemon laws are tied in with the particular state's inspection requirement. Depending on the state, safety inspections may cover a number of items on a car, including the brakes, tires, seatbelts, lights, etc. If the car fails this safety inspection within a certain time period after the purchase, and the cost of repair exceeds the state's set amount, which is often computed as a percentage of the purchase price, the consumer may be able to recover under the state's lemon law.

Due to variations in state lemon law requirements, the reader is advised to check their own state's lemon law statute for specific provisions.

A table of state lemon law statute citations is set forth at Appendix 1 and a directory of state lemon law websites is set forth at Appendix 2.

In addition, your state attorney general's office, consumer protection agency, and state lemon law contacts can also provide you with copies of your state's lemon law.

A directory of state attorney general offices is set forth at Appendix 3; a directory of state consumer protection agencies is set forth at Appendix 4; and a directory of state lemon law contacts is set forth at Appendix 5.

COVERED VEHICLES

All state lemon laws cover new cars provided the car is purchased for personal, family or household use. About half of the states have a lemon law that covers leased cars, but only Arizona, Connecticut, Hawaii, Maine, Massachusetts, Minnesota, New Jersey, New York and Rhode Island have lemon laws that cover used cars. However, if your car is a "Certified Used Vehicle"—i.e., it came with a manufacturer warranty— it is generally considered a "new" car and thus covered under the lemon law. Most states cover the drive train portion of a motor home or recreational vehicle—i.e., that part of the vehicle not used for dwelling purposes. State lemon laws do not cover trucks or off-road vehicles. A few states cover motorcycles.

A table of vehicles covered under state lemon laws is set forth at Appendix 6.

LEMON LAW COVERAGE PERIODS

The manufacturer's warranty that comes with your car when you buy it covers routine repairs and problems that can be fixed. If you have a problem with your car and you return it to the dealer, your car will probably be repaired under the manufacturer's warranty provided it falls within the warranty period, which may be expressed as a certain time period or mileage, whichever comes first—e.g., 1 year or 12,000 miles. If the dealer or manufacturer does not honor the terms of the warranty, you can generally sue them for breach of warranty. This is different from the recourse available under a state lemon law.

As set forth above, state lemon laws cover problems that cannot be fixed after a reasonable number of repair attempts. Most lemon laws set forth their own coverage periods—also referred to as "lemon law rights" periods—during which the manufacturer must fix your car if it turns out to be a lemon. In some states, the lemon law coverage period is the same as the manufacturer's warranty. Some states extend that coverage period for cars that qualify as lemons.

A table of coverage periods under state lemon laws is set forth at Appendix 7.

As an example, following is an excerpt from New York's lemon law, which covers both new and used cars.

The New York New Car Lemon Law

Pursuant to New York State General Business Law, Section 198-a, the New Car Lemon Law provides a legal remedy for consumers who buy or lease a new car and certain used cars, from automobile dealers, which turn out to be defective. This right cannot be waived in the contract, and any contract clause that attempts to waive this right is void.

A car is covered under this provision if:

1. The car was covered by the manufacturer's new car warranty at the time of original delivery; and

2. The car was purchased, leased or transferred within the earlier of the first 18,000 miles or two years from the date of original delivery; and

3. The car either: (a) was purchased, leased or transferred in New York; or (b) is presently registered in New York; and

4. The car is primarily used for personal purposes.

If the car does not conform to the terms of the written warranty, and the consumer is still experiencing problems with the vehicle after a reasonable number of repair attempts by the manufacturer or its authorized dealer during the earlier of the first 18,000 miles or two years, the consumer is entitled to a full refund or a comparable replacement car.

The New York Used Car Lemon Law

Pursuant to New York State General Business Law, Section 198-b, the Used Car Lemon Law provides a legal remedy for consumers who buy or lease certain covered used cars, from automobile dealers, which turn out to be defective. This right also cannot be waived in the contract, and any contract clause that attempts to waive this right is void. Furthermore, a dealer is prohibited from selling a covered used car in an "as is" condition.

A used car is covered under this provision if:

1. It was purchased, leased or transferred after the earlier of (a) 18,000 miles of operation or (b) two years from the date of original delivery; and

2. It was purchased or leased from a New York dealer; and

3. It had a purchase price or lease value of at least $1,500; and

4. It had been driven less than 100,000 miles at the time of purchase or lease; and

5. It is primarily used for personal purposes.

A used car purchased or leased with 18,000 miles or less, and within two years from the date of original delivery, is covered by the New Car Lemon Law, as set forth above. The law also covers persons to whom the used car was transferred by the purchaser during the used car lemon law warranty period. The law does not cover the private sale of automobiles.

The Used Car Lemon Law requires the dealer to give the consumer a written warranty which states that the dealer must repair, free of charge, any defects in certain specified covered parts. If the consumer is still experiencing problems with the vehicle after a reasonable number of repair attempts, the consumer is entitled to a full refund.

The warranty period on a covered used car is based on the mileage at the time of purchase or lease, as follows:

1. Cars with 18,001 to 36,000 miles at the time of purchase or lease are covered until the earlier of 90 days or after 4,000 miles have elapsed;

2. Cars with 36,001 to 79,999 miles at the time of purchase or lease are covered until the earlier of 60 days or after 3,000 miles have elapsed;

3. Cars with 80,000 to 100,000 miles at the time of purchase or lease are covered until the earlier of 30 days or after 1,000 miles have elapsed.

The warranty period is extended for each day that the car is in the shop being repaired.

SECRET WARRANTIES

If a car manufacturer discovers that a particular car make/model has problems that affect a large number of its cars, the manufacturer may establish a "secret warranty" or "warranty adjustment" program. Such a program extends the length of the original manufacturer's warranty, e.g. for six months. During the extension period, the manufacturer will continue to repair those cars that have exhibited persistent problems. Manufacturers establish these programs in order to avoid recalls of the problem cars and the attendant bad publicity such widespread recalls cause.

If a manufacturer decides to establish an extended warranty program, the manufacturer may send a letter to owners of the problem cars, advising them of the warranty extension. Most states, however, do not require the manufacturer to notify the owners of the problem cars, and the burden is on the consumer to find out whether there is a warranty extension on their car. The only states that require manufacturers to advise problem car owners of a warranty extension program are California, Connecticut, Virginia and Wisconsin.

CRITERIA FOR DETERMINING WHETHER YOUR CAR IS A LEMON

Different states have developed different criteria for determining whether a car a lemon, therefore, the reader is advised to check the law of his or her jurisdiction for specific information not included in this almanac.

Repair Attempts

A typical lemon law statute gives the dealer one to two attempts to repair a serious safety defect, such as brake failures, and three to four chances to repair any other defect that renders the car unusable. Another method of determining whether the dealer has had a reasonable chance to repair the car is the number of days the car is inoperable, e.g., 30 cumulative days during a one-year interval.

A table of repair attempts and intervals under state lemon laws is set forth at Appendix 8.

Same Defect

In order to qualify as a lemon, the dealer must be unable to repair the identical chronic defect in the car. For example, if you have a problem with your brakes, and the dealer repeatedly tries to fix the brakes on a number of occasions, your car would likely be covered under the lemon law because of this chronic defect. However, if you have different problems with your car, such as the brakes fail one time, and then you have a transmission problem, your car would probably not qualify as a lemon.

THE LEMON LAW PRESUMPTION

Some states, such as California, have a "lemon law presumption." Under this presumption, any defect or condition that substantially impairs the use, value or safety of your vehicle under warranty, that you have tried to have repaired by an authorized dealer, entitles you to seek a refund or replacement under the state's lemon law, even if the manufacturer continues to say it cannot find a problem. The legal presumption recognizes that if you purchased a new car, you have the right to rely on its dependability and safety.

For example, California's lemon law contains guidelines so the consumer can make a reasonable legal "presumption" that the manufacturer has had enough time or opportunity to repair the car but still did not fix it, as follows:

1. You have taken your vehicle to an authorized dealer four or more times about the same problem, or your vehicle has been out of service for 30 days or more because of any number of problems. The 30 days do not have to be consecutive. If the defect is likely to cause death or serious injury to you or your passengers if you drive the car, you can ask for a refund or replacement after only two unsuccessful repair attempts.

2. The four repair attempts or 30 days out of service have occurred within the first 18 months that you own your car or the first 18,000 miles, whichever happens first.

3. The problems are covered by the warranty and substantially impair the use, value or safety of the vehicle.

4. You must directly notify the manufacturer about the problem in writing if you want to use the "four times" repair requirement and if the manufacturer requires such notification in the warranty materials or owner's manual.

If you meet any or all of the foregoing guidelines, you have met the legal presumption requirement, and it is likely that you will receive a refund or replacement under the lemon law.

Nevertheless, presumptions can be challenged and proven not to be true. For example, if the manufacturer can prove that it has not had a reasonable opportunity to repair your car, you may not be entitled to a refund or a replacement vehicle. In addition, if the manufacturer can prove that you abused the car, damaged it in an accident or made an alteration to the vehicle that voided the warranty, the state lemon law may not apply.

PURCHASING A PREVIOUSLY RETURNED LEMON CAR

A car that has been previously returned because it was deemed to be a lemon car can be resold or released, under certain conditions. In general, the manufacturer must provide the purchaser with a 12-month or 12,000 mile warranty from the date of resale, and must also provide a statement advising the purchaser that the car had been returned to the manufacturer because it was a lemon car.

The International Association of Lemon Law Administrators (IALLA) is calling on the federal government to adopt a tracking system for all defective new vehicles deemed "lemons" to prevent consumers from being unwittingly stuck with problem cars.

CONSUMER PROTECTION ORGANIZATIONS

As set forth below, there are a number of private and governmental organizations at the local, state and federal level which are designed to assist the consumer, and/or to protect and advocate for the consumer's rights. If you are having a problem with the dealer who sold you your car, you can usually obtain helpful information and advice from these organizations.

National Consumer Organizations

There are many private and voluntary national organizations whose missions are defined as consumer assistance, protection and/or advocacy. Among other things, these organizations assist consumers with their problems and concerns. However, they have no enforcement authority.

Most of these organizations develop and distribute consumer education and information materials. Some of these organizations are professional associations primarily or exclusively concerned with improving consumer protection or customer service. Many of these organizations advocate for consumer interests before government, the courts, and the news media.

A directory of national consumer organizations is set forth at Appendix 9.

State and Local Consumer Protection Offices

State and local consumer protection offices work to resolve consumer complaints and also distribute consumer education information. Some offices investigate and prosecute offenders of consumer laws, as well

well as mediate disputes. They also promote consumer protection legislation and advocate for the consumer.

City and county consumer offices are familiar with local businesses and local ordinances and state laws. If there is no local consumer office in the area, the consumer should contact their state consumer office. State offices, sometimes in a separate department of consumer affairs or the attorney general or governor's office, are familiar with state laws and look for statewide patterns of problems. Many offices distribute consumer materials specifically geared to state laws and local issues.

A directory of state consumer protection agencies is set forth at Appendix 4.

Better Business Bureaus

The Better Business Bureau (BBB) is a non-profit organization supported primarily by local businesses. The focus of the BBB is to promote an ethical marketplace by encouraging honest advertising and selling practices. The Council of Better Business Bureaus (CBBB) is the umbrella organization for the BBB branches, and is supported by national companies and the BBB branches.

A national directory of Better Business Bureaus is set forth at Appendix 10.

The BBB offers the consumer a variety of services, including: (1) general information on products or services, (2) business reliability reports; (3) background information on businesses, organizations and charities; (4) consumer education programs; and (5) arbitration and mediation services.

The BBB usually requests that a complaint be submitted in writing so that an accurate record exists of the dispute. The BBB will then take up the complaint with the company involved. If the complaint cannot be satisfactorily resolved through communication with the business, the BBB may offer an alternative dispute settlement process, such as mediation or arbitration. However, the BBBs do not judge or rate individual products or brands or give legal advice.

If you need help with a consumer question or complaint, call your local BBB to ask about its services. Some bureaus that provide information via 1-900 telephone numbers charge a fee. You can also contact the BBB online for consumer fraud and scam alerts, and information about BBB programs, services and locations.

The U.S. Office of Consumer Affairs

The United States Office of Consumer Affairs publishes a Consumer Resource Handbook which provides helpful information and resource directories for the consumer. Copies may be obtained by contacting the U.S. Office of Consumer Affairs, 750 17th Street, N.W., Washington, DC 20006-4607.

Automobile Manufacturer Consumer Relations Departments

Many companies have organized in-house consumer relations departments to address consumer concerns and help resolve consumer complaints. Even if you decide to go back to the dealer to make a complaint, you should also let the consumer relations department at the company's headquarters know about the problem. Most automobile manufacturers have organized national or regional offices to handle consumer complaints that are not resolved by the local car dealer. You can find out whether a certain automobile manufacturer has a consumer relations department by contacting that company's headquarters.

ADDITIONAL LEGISLATION

In addition to state lemon laws, those engaged in the business of selling automobiles are subject to numerous additional state and federal laws, such as the federal Magnuson-Moss Warranty Act, the federal Odometer Act, and Article 2 of the Uniform Commercial Code, which covers contracts dealing with the sale of defective products. In fact, most state lemon laws are based upon the federal Magnuson-Moss Warranty Act, which is discussed below.

A consumer may also find a remedy within their state's warranty laws and consumer protection statute prohibiting unfair and deceptive acts and practices. If you have a defective car that is not covered under your state's lemon law, you may still have recourse under these laws. Therefore, the reader is advised to check the law of his or her own jurisdiction for additional protection.

Magnuson-Moss Warranty Act

Almost all state lemon law statutes are based on the federal Magnuson-Moss Warranty Act, which makes breach of warranty a violation of federal law. The Magnuson-Moss Warranty Act is a federal law passed in 1975 that governs consumer product warranties. The Act protects the buyer of any product that costs more than $25 and comes with an express written warranty.

The Act requires manufacturers and sellers of consumer products to provide consumers with detailed information about warranty coverage. In addition, it affects both the rights of consumers and the obligations of warrantors under written warranties. The Act promotes timely and complete performance of warranty obligations for any product that does not perform as it should.

The Act gives consumers considerable rights in dealing with manufacturers and car-dealers of lemon automobiles. This law guarantees a car buyer that certain minimum requirements of warranties must be met, and provides for disclosure of warranties before purchase. Under the Act, if the product—the lemon car—has a written warranty, and if any part of the product—or the product itself—is considered defective, the warrantor must permit the buyer the choice of either a refund or replacement of the product. The Act also provides that the consumer may sue the manufacturer to enforce his or her rights.

The text of the Magnusson-Moss Warranty Act is set forth at Appendix 11.

Disclosure Rule

Under the Act's Disclosure Rule, written warranties must be available for the consumer to read before buying. The written warranty must be clear, easy to read, and contain certain specified items of information about its coverage. There are five basic provisions of coverage that the warranty must set forth.

1. Scope of Coverage—The warranty must describe what is and what is not covered

2. Length of Coverage—If coverage begins at some point in time other than the purchase date, your warranty must state the time or event that begins the coverage. Also, the warranty must make it clear when coverage ends if some particular event would terminate it, e.g. upon transfer to another person.

3. Remedies—The warranty must contain an explanation of the remedy the warrantor offers under the warranty, e.g., repair or replacement of the product; or a refund of the purchase price, etc.

4. Method of Obtaining Warranty Service—The warranty must tell consumers who they can go to for warranty service and how to reach the authorized repair service.

5. State Law—The warranty must also explain how state law may affect the consumer's rights under the warranty. The boilerplate language adopted is "This warranty gives you specific legal rights, and you may also have other rights which vary from state to state."

Remedies Under the Act

The Act makes it easier for consumers to take an unresolved warranty problem to court by making breach of warranty a violation of federal law, and by allowing consumers to recover court costs and reasonable attorneys' fees. This means that if the warrantor loses a lawsuit for breach of either a written or an implied warranty, they may have to pay the consumer's costs for bringing the suit, including lawyer's fees.

Nevertheless, the Act encourages companies to use less formal—and therefore less costly— alternatives to legal proceedings in order to settle warranty disputes with their customers. Such alternatives—known as dispute resolution methods—often can be used to settle warranty complaints before they reach litigation.

Alternative dispute resolution methods may be run by an impartial third party, such as the Better Business Bureau, or by company employees whose only job is to administer the informal dispute resolution system. The impartial third party uses conciliation, mediation, or arbitration to settle warranty disputes.

Although the Act makes it easier for a consumer to sue for breach of warranty, the Act also allows warrantors to include a provision that requires the consumer to try to resolve warranty disputes by means of the informal dispute resolution mechanism before they are permitted to file a lawsuit in court. However, the chosen mechanism procedure must:

1. Be adequately funded and staffed to resolve all disputes quickly;

2. Be available free of charge to consumers;

3. Be able to settle disputes independently, without influence from the parties involved;

4. Follow written procedures;

5. Inform both parties when it receives notice of a dispute;

6. Gather, investigate, and organize all information necessary to decide each dispute fairly and quickly;

7. Provide each party an opportunity to present its side, to submit supporting materials, and to rebut points made by the other party;

8. Allow oral presentations, but only if both parties agree;

9. Inform both parties of the decision and the reasons supporting it within 40 days of receiving notice of a dispute;

10. Issue decisions that are not binding where either party must be free to take the dispute to court if dissatisfied with the decision;

11. Keep complete records on all disputes; and

12. Be audited annually for compliance with the Rule.

Nevertheless, the company does not have to comply with the Dispute Resolution Rule if it does not require consumers to use an alternate dispute resolution method before bringing a lawsuit in court under the Magnuson-Moss Warranty Act.

CHAPTER 2:
PREPARING YOUR LEMON LAW CLAIM

FOLLOW PROCEDURES

If you want to prevail on your lemon law claim, it is crucial that you prepare carefully. You are up against manufacturers and dealerships that pose a strong opposition. You must keep detailed records, and follow the prescribed procedures required by the law. Depending on the particular state, this may include (1) providing proper notice of the defect and giving the manufacturer a reasonable opportunity to repair the car; (2) asking the manufacturer to give you a replacement car or refund; and, if the manufacturer refuses, (3) utilizing lemon law arbitration programs before going to court. In any event, your success depends in large part on the documentation you provide in support of your claim.

DOCUMENT YOUR LEMON LAW CLAIM

You must provide evidence in order to prevail in your lemon law claim. Gather all of the information and documentation that proves your claim. Types of information and documentation that will help support your claim include those listed below.

Repair Orders

When you bring your car to the dealer for repair, make sure you provide the details of the car's problem on the repair or work order. The repair order documents what you asked the mechanic to do. You should describe the problem in exactly the same language each time you return to the dealer to get the same defect repaired. If you don't, you risk losing your rights under the lemon law because the repeated repair attempts must be for the same defect or condition.

Repair Invoices

In order to recover under the lemon law, you must document the repair attempts. This is important because you must demonstrate that you made the number of repair attempts required under your state's lemon law. You should keep a copy of every repair invoice or receipt you are given. The repair invoice documents what the mechanic actually did to try and repair the defect. This is particularly important if you are out of town and must have the car repaired at another repair shop. If the service department does not automatically provide you with an invoice after each repair attempt, you should request a copy so you can demonstrate that an attempted repair was made for the same defect or condition.

Keep Notes of Conversations

You should write down the names of all persons you speak with about the problem or defect, including the mechanic who works on the car, customer service representatives, service department personnel, etc. Note the date, time and the specifics of what was discussed during each conversation. Your complaints should always be made in writing, and you should keep a copy of your complaint in your file.

Vehicle Repair Log

You should maintain a vehicle repair log in order to adequately demonstrate the number of times you had to take your car in to be repaired, and the details of the repair attempt. This way, when you approach the manufacturer for a replacement car or refund, it will be easy to explain the problems you have been having, as well as your consistent but unsuccessful efforts to get the condition repaired. The repair log is a detailed summary of the attempted repairs performed on your car. Your repair log should show the dates, mileage, and complaints for every visit you've made to the dealer to have your vehicle repaired. Your repair log should note whether or not the defect could be repaired.

Following is information which should be included in your repair log.

1. Vehicle information, such as make, model, license plate number, vehicle identification number, etc.

2. The date you purchased your vehicle.

3. The odometer reading as of the date you took possession of your car.

4. The dates and actual mileage for each time you took your vehicle in for repair.

5. The repair completion dates and actual mileage for each time you picked up your vehicle.

6. The name of the dealer or authorized repair shop where your vehicle is taken.

7. The repair order number printed on the repair work order.

8. A description of the work requested or a detailed description of the problem that needs to be repaired. Again, each time you bring your car in for the same problem, you must make sure you describe the problem identically on the work order. Don't leave it up to the service technician to describe the problem.

9. A description of the actual work performed as shown on the invoice you receive when you pick up your car. If the dealer refuses to give you an invoice—e.g., because the vehicle was under warranty and there was no charge—make a note of the dealer's refusal in your repair log.

10. The cost of repairs, including incidental charges such as towing or car rental. Attach copies of all receipts.

If the problem or defect is not corrected, note that in your repair log and bring the car back to the dealer for another repair attempt. Make sure you note the details of the new repair attempt in your repair log.

A sample repair log is set forth at Appendix 12.

Technical Service Bulletins

Technical Service Bulletins are alerts sent from the manufacturer to the dealership concerning defects found in certain car models. The bulletins advise dealers of repairs that should be made on the affected cars. Although these bulletins are not made public, you can obtain copies of any bulletins released for your particular make and model car from the dealer. The National Highway and Traffic Safety Administration (NHTSA) also maintains a list of bulletins. Contact information for the NHTSA is:

National Highway and Traffic Safety Administration

Telephone: 800-424-9393

Website: www.nhtsa.dot.gov.

A sample technical service bulletin published by Mazda concerning the brakes on the 2001-2002 Miata is set forth at Appendix 13.

Maintenance Records

In order to support your claim under your state's lemon law, you will need to show that you properly maintained your car according to the

---

manufacturer's recommendations. Otherwise, a claim may be made that the car's problems were caused by your negligence instead of a manufacturing defect. Routine maintenance includes oil changes, engine tune-ups, checking fluids, rotating tires, etc. The Federal Consumer Information Center (FCIC) has published a car maintenance checklist and more extensive list of maintenance tips.

The FCIC car maintenance checklist is set forth at Appendix 14.

Purchase/Lease Documents

In order to properly calculate your refund, as set forth in Chapter 3, you need your original purchase or lease documents. These documents will assist you in documenting how much you paid for your car, the down payment, taxes, and other expenses and fees.

NOTICE OF DEFECT

Generally, if a car has been repaired a reasonable number of times for the same defect, within the statute's coverage period, and the defect persists, the car will qualify as a lemon and the consumer will have recourse under the state's lemon law. In some states, if the defect is serious enough to cause bodily injury, one failed repair attempt is enough to consider your car a lemon. A car may also be considered a lemon if it is out of commission for a certain number of days—e.g., 30 days—within a certain time period.

In order to recover under the state's lemon law and document your case, you must, however, notify the manufacturer about the defect, and give the manufacturer a reasonable opportunity to repair the car. In some states, you must also notify the dealership. Notification must be made in writing in order to properly document your claim, therefore, it is a waste of time to call the customer service line and complain.

For example, under the Iowa lemon law, the consumer must advise the manufacturer of the following: (1) whether the car has been out of service for at least 20 cumulative days for repair; and/or (2) whether there have been three or more attempts to repair the same defect or condition; and/or (3) whether the car has been in the repair shop for a defect that was likely to cause death or serious bodily injury. The notice of defect also requests the manufacturer to make a "final attempt to correct the continuing substantial defect(s) or condition(s)." The manufacturer may offer to extend the warranty and attempt to repair the car a few more times.

A copy of the Iowa Motor Vehicle Defect Notification form requesting a final repair attempt is set forth at Appendix 15.

REQUEST FOR REPLACEMENT OR REFUND

If you have satisfied your state's lemon law requirements, and the car is unable to be repaired after the specified number of repair attempts, you should send a letter to the manufacturer requesting a replacement car or a refund. In your letter, provide the name and address of the dealership where you purchased the car, as well as a description of the car, including the year, make/model, and vehicle identification (VIN) number.

In your letter, describe the problem you have been having with the car, and the number of repair attempts that have been made by the dealer to correct the defect. Advise the manufacturer that you will have no choice but to pursue your remedies under the state's lemon law if the manufacturer does not comply with your request for a replacement car or refund. Attach copies of your maintenance records; repair log, including invoices and work orders; purchase/lease documents; and any correspondence you have concerning the defect. Keep the original documents in a safe place.

Your letter should be sent to the manufacturer's address as set forth in the owner's manual. By law, manufacturers are required to provide their mailing address in a clear and conspicuous manner in all owners' manuals. Send the letter by certified mail, and request a return receipt so you have proof that the manufacturer received your letter. Also, keep a copy of the letter for your own records.

If you are given a replacement car, it should be of comparable value to the car you purchased, and you should also request reimbursement of your repair costs. If the manufacturer agrees to give you a refund, it should include the purchase price, finance charges, taxes, and repair costs.

If the manufacturer refuses to honor your request, you will have to proceed to arbitration and/or litigation, depending on your state's law. Some state lemon laws allow a manufacturer to require the consumer to submit to arbitration before going to court.

Lemon law arbitration is discussed more fully in Chapter 4 of this almanac.

CHAPTER 3:
YOUR REMEDIES UNDER STATE LEMON LAWS

IN GENERAL

State lemon laws generally entitle the consumer to a replacement car or a refund if the car they purchased is unable to be repaired. You may also be able to recover the costs associated with the purchase, such as registration and titling fees, finance charges, sales tax, etc. You should also request reimbursement for any repair costs. However, if you continue to drive the car while your claim is pending, the law may permit the seller to deduct a certain amount from any refund you are awarded based on the mileage you put on the car.

OBTAINING A REPLACEMENT VEHICLE

Lemon laws generally define a "replacement motor vehicle" as a motor vehicle which is identical or reasonably equivalent to the motor vehicle being replaced, as the motor vehicle being replaced existed at the time of acquisition. "Reasonably equivalent to the motor vehicle being replaced" means that the manufacturer's suggested retail price (MSRP) of the replacement vehicle shall not exceed 105 percent of the MSRP of the vehicle being replaced.

In addition to the replacement vehicle, you may also recover the following items.

Collateral Charges

You may recover the amount of any reasonable "collateral charges," such as interest paid on your loan or lease as of the date of repurchase, window tinting, extended warranty, additional items installed in or on the vehicle, etc.

Incidental Charges

You may recover the amount of any reasonable "incidental charges," such as postage, long distance calls, rental car, towing, warranty deductibles or repair charges, etc., that were incurred as a direct result of the defect or condition that substantially impaired the use, value or safety of the vehicle.

Reasonable Offset For Use

You must pay the manufacturer the reasonable offset for your use of the car, as computed below, in order to obtain the replacement motor vehicle.

Substitution Under Existing Loan or Lease

If you financed your car and still owe a balance on the loan, you should contact your lender to find out whether you will be able to substitute your replacement car for the original car under your existing loan, and if you will incur additional costs.

If you leased your car, you should contact your lessor to find out whether you will be able to substitute your replacement car for the original car under your existing lease, and if you will incur additional costs. Further, the lessor cannot charge you an early termination penalty for the replacement car.

CALCULATING YOUR REFUND

If you prefer to receive a refund instead of a replacement car, you need to know the basic manner in which a refund is calculated. Following are typical refund calculation guidelines as set forth in Florida's lemon law.

Reasonable Offset For Use

Under this provision, you are charged an offset for your use of the car, which is based on the mileage you put on the car as of the date of a settlement agreement or arbitration hearing, whichever occurs first. In the case of a refund award, your cash award is reduced by the amount of the offset. In the case of a replacement car award, you must pay the offset to the manufacturer to obtain the replacement car.

The formula used to determine the offset is as follows:

(1) Purchase Price (reduced by any manufacturer rebate to the consumer and exclusive of debt from any other transaction); (2) multiplied by the mileage attributable to the consumer (reduced by mileage at delivery and other non-consumer mileage) as of the date of settlement or an arbitration hearing; (3) divided by 120,000, or 60,000 if the vehicle is a recreational vehicle (RV).

EXAMPLE: If your purchase price was $24,000.00 and your mileage at the applicable date was 20,000 miles, your offset would be $4,000.00.

EXAMPLE: (RV): If your purchase price was $50,000.00 and your mileage at the applicable date was 10,000 miles, your offset would be $8,333.33.

Obtaining Your Refund

If you request a refund, the amount is calculated depending upon whether you financed the purchase, leased the vehicle or paid cash.

If You Financed the Purchase of Your Vehicle

If you financed the purchase of your car by borrowing all or a portion of the purchase price, your finance institution (e.g. bank, credit union or finance company) may have a lien on the car. In these situations, if a refund is awarded, you and the lien holder are paid according to your respective interests in the car. This usually means that you are awarded the amounts you paid toward the purchase of the car, reduced by the offset for use, and the manufacturer pays off the loan on the car.

Following are examples of items that you may recover:

Cash Down Payment

You may recover the amount of any cash down payment less any portion of the down payment attributable to a manufacturer rebate, if any.

Periodic Payments

You may recover the amount of periodic payments, including principal and interest, that you made on the loan as of the date of repurchase of the vehicle by the manufacturer.

Collateral Charges

You may recover the amount of any reasonable "collateral charges" in addition to the cash down payment that were not financed, such as window tinting, government fees, extended warranty, additional items installed in the vehicle, etc.

Trade-In Allowance

You may recover the amount of any allowance for a trade-in car. This means the net trade-in allowance in the purchase agreement, if this is acceptable to you and the manufacturer. If this amount is not acceptable, then the trade-in allowance will be 100% of the retail value of the trade-in car as depicted in the NADA Official Used Car Guide in effect at the time of the trade-in. The Manufacturer must produce the applicable NADA guide.

The net trade-in allowance set forth in the purchase agreement will likely be rejected if you traded in a car on which a debt was still owed to a lien holder, and the dealer "inflated" or increased the allowance for the trade-in to account for this debt. In this event, the Arbitration Board will look to the retail value of the trade-in car, as reflected in the NADA Official Used Car Guide which was in effect at the time of the trade-in, and that figure will be reduced by the amount of debt you owed on the trade-in car when it was traded in.

If the NADA Guide provides for increasing the retail value for such things as low mileage, and specified accessories, and the trade-in car had these items, the Board may utilize the higher retail value.

Use of the NADA Guide in these circumstances could result in the trade-in allowance being a negative amount, which may further reduce the amount of money awarded to you. However, if there was minimal, or no debt remaining on the trade-in, and the net trade-in allowance given by the selling dealer was less than the retail value in the NADA guide, use of the NADA retail value may increase the amount of your award.

You should research the trade-in issue prior to entering into settlement negotiations, or prior to an arbitration hearing, so you are able to make an informed election with regard to the trade-in allowance.

Incidental Charges

You may recover the amount of any reasonable "incidental charges," such as postage, long distance calls, rental car, towing, warranty deductibles or repair charges, etc., that were incurred as a direct result of the defect or condition that substantially impaired the use, value or safety of the vehicle.

Final Calculation

To calculate the total amount of your refund:

1. Add the (1) cash down payment; (2) periodic payments; and (3) collateral charges.

2. Add or subtract the trade-in allowance depending on whether the allowance is positive or negative.

3. Subtract the reasonable offset for use.

4. Add the incidental charges.

This calculation should give you an estimate of your portion of a refund. The lien holder should be paid the balance owed or payoff on the loan as of the date the car is repurchased by the Manufacturer.

If You Leased Your Vehicle

If you leased your vehicle, then you are the "lessee" and the entity to which you send your payments every month is, most likely, the "lessor." Under the lemon law, refunds are made to the lessor and lessee. The lessee receives the "lessee cost"—the aggregate deposit and rental payments previously paid by the lessee. The lessor receives the "lease price" less the lessee cost. In addition, the lessor is not permitted to charge a penalty for early termination of the lease.

Following are examples of items that may be included in the "lessee cost."

Security Deposit

You may recover the amount of any security deposit paid at lease signing.

Out-Of-Pocket Costs

You may recover any other costs paid out-of-pocket to obtain the lease, such as service fees, pro-rated taxes, government fees, first monthly payment in advance, etc.

Total Lease Payments

You may recover the total amount of lease payments made as of the date of repurchase of the vehicle;

Collateral Charges

You may recover the amount of any reasonable "collateral charges" that were not included in the amounts paid at lease signing or incorporated in your monthly lease payments, such as window tinting, government fees, extended warranty, additional items installed in or on the car, etc.

Trade-In Allowance

You may recover the amount of any allowance for a trade-in car as set forth above.

Incidental Charges

You may recover the amount of any reasonable "incidental charges," such as postage, long distance calls, rental car, towing, warranty deductibles or repair charges, etc., that were incurred as a direct result of the defect or condition that substantially impaired the use, value or safety of the vehicle.

Final Calculation

To calculate the total amount of your refund:

1. Add the (1) security deposit; (2) out-of-pocket costs; (3) lease payments; and (4) collateral charges.

2. Add or subtract the trade-in allowance depending on whether the allowance is positive or negative.

3. Subtract the reasonable offset for use.

4. Add the incidental charges.

This calculation should give you an estimate of your portion of a refund. The manufacturer should pay the lessor the "lease price" less "lessee cost" as computed above.

If You Paid Cash to Purchase Your Vehicle

If you paid cash to purchase your vehicle, following are items you may recover.

Total Cash Price

You may recover the total cash paid to acquire the vehicle, reduced by any manufacturer rebate, if applicable.

Collateral Charges

You may recover the amount of any reasonable "collateral charges" not included in the cash paid to acquire the vehicle, such as window tinting, government fees, extended warranty, additional items installed in the vehicle, etc.

Trade-In Allowance

You may recover the amount of any allowance for a trade-in vehicle as set forth above.

Incidental Charges

You may recover the amount of any reasonable "incidental charges," such as postage, long distance calls, rental car, towing, warranty deductibles or repair charges, etc., that were incurred as a direct result of the defect or condition that substantially impaired the use, value or safety of the vehicle.

Final Calculation

To calculate the total amount of your refund:

1. Add the (1) total cash price; and (2) collateral charges.

2. Add or subtract the trade-in allowance depending on whether the allowance is positive or negative.

3. Subtract the reasonable offset for use.

4. Add the incidental charges.

CHAPTER 4:
LEMON LAW ARBITRATION

IN GENERAL

If the manufacturer refuses to give you a replacement car or a refund, you can try using the manufacturer's in-house arbitration procedure, if there is one in place. Various auto manufacturers and dealers have established their own arbitration programs. In some states, the law requires you to participate in any state-certified in-house arbitration proceeding before you are permitted to sue in court, provided the in-house proceeding complies with the state's lemon law and the federal regulations. "State-certified" generally means that the manufacturer's arbitration procedure meets certain state and federal requirements; however, it does not mean that the program is administered or sponsored by the state.

Arbitration is state-run in Connecticut, Florida, Georgia, Hawaii, Maine, Massachusetts, New Hampshire, New Jersey, New York, Texas, Vermont and Washington. In other states, arbitration programs are run by the manufacturer, the Better Business Bureau or the National Automobile Dealers Association.

If you are permitted to choose your own arbitrator, it is advisable to use a Better Business Bureau arbitration program or a state consumer protection arbitration program instead of the manufacturer's in-house program.

A directory of automobile dispute resolution programs is set forth at Appendix 16.

In some states, you are required to first use the manufacturer's in-house arbitration program to try and resolve the dispute. If you are unable to resolve your problem at this level, you can then try to resolve your lemon law claim in the state-run arbitration program.

For example, New York has established its own Lemon Law Arbitration Program for both new and used cars. The law permits an auto manufacturer to establish its own state-certified arbitration program and require consumers to participate in an in-house arbitration proceeding before the consumer is permitted to sue in court. However, the decisions reached in the in-house programs are not binding on the consumer. After complying with the in-house program, the consumer is entitled to submit their dispute to the American Arbitration Association (AAA) under the New York Lemon Law Arbitration Program.

The New York program is administered by the AAA under regulations issued by the state Attorney General. In order to initiate arbitration under the New York program, the consumer must file a request for arbitration with the Attorney General's office. Upon review of the request, the Attorney General's office determines whether the consumer is eligible for arbitration under the law.

A sample request for arbitration under the New York Lemon Law Arbitration Program is set forth at Appendix XX.

If the consumer's claim is deemed eligible for arbitration, the request is forwarded to the AAA, who contacts the consumer. The consumer is required to forward a filing fee to the AAA, who then appoints an arbitrator and schedules a hearing. The consumer has a right to an oral hearing before an arbitrator who is specially trained in the lemon law. The consumer may request that the hearing be conducted by review of the documentation only. However if the manufacturer objects to a "documents only" hearing, an oral hearing must be held.

The decisions rendered in the New York program are binding on both parties, subject only to limited judicial review under New York law. The manufacturer must comply with the arbitrator's decision within 30 days or face penalties.

THE ARBITRATION PROCEEDING

Arbitration is a process whereby an impartial third party, known as an arbitrator, listens to both sides of the dispute and issues a decision. Arbitration is similar to—but less formal than—a trial before a judge. In general, arbitration is informal, less expensive and less time consuming than going to court.

During the arbitration hearing, both the consumer and the car manufacturer present their arguments to the arbitrator. The arbitration hearing generally begins with opening statements, much like a trial. Each party then briefly states their positions, what their case will prove, and the outcome to which they believe they are entitled. The consumer will then present his or her case by producing evidence, such as the consumer's documentation supporting the lemon law claim, and any witnesses. For example, the consumer in a lemon law arbitration hearing should consider bringing an independent auto mechanic who has inspected the car to testify about the defective condition.

The witnesses may be questioned by either side. After the consumer finishes presenting his or her case, the auto manufacturer will respond by presenting its case in the same manner as the consumer. After both parties have presented their sides of the dispute, each party can sum up their case in a closing statement.

Although the arbitration hearing appears to parallel a trial, the parties to the arbitration hearing forego certain rights they would have had in a trial in order to expedite the arbitration process. For example, the rules of evidence are relaxed in arbitration, making it easy to enter into evidence items that would never be permitted at trial.

The arbitrator's decision can be either binding or nonbinding, according to agreement by the parties. Depending on the state, the arbitrator's decision may not be binding on the consumer, although it may be binding on the manufacturer. Thus, if you are not satisfied with the arbitrator's decision, you usually have the right to file a complaint in court. Some states, such as Florida, have an additional state-run level of arbitration where you can file your claim if you are dissatisfied with the outcome of the manufacturer's arbitration procedure, as discussed below. Other states may allow you to go directly to court instead of arbitration.

If the arbitrator's decision is not binding, it cannot be enforced in court. A binding agreement is enforceable in court just like a contract. If the parties agree to a binding decision, they can also agree to set limits on the arbitrator's decision—e.g., a high/low agreement. In a high/low agreement, the parties establish a minimum and maximum amount. If the arbitrator's decision exceeds the maximum, the manufacturer is only obligated to pay the agreed maximum amount. If the arbitrator's decision is lower than the minimum, the manufacturer must pay at least the agreed minimum amount.

Arbitration is an informal procedure; therefore, you do not need to be represented by an attorney provided you are organized and prepare properly. However, if you feel uncomfortable representing yourself, find an attorney who is experienced in lemon law cases to represent you at the arbitration hearing.

PREPARING FOR THE ARBITRATION HEARING

In order to prepare for your arbitration hearing, you should gather all of the documentation related to your claim, as discussed in Chapter 2 of this almanac. This includes your warranty, repair log, inspection reports, technical service bulletins, etc. You should make copies of these documents in order to submit them to the arbitrator at the hearing.

In generally, your arbitration hearing must be held within a certain number of days—e.g., 40—after you file your request for arbitration. The manufacturer must then comply with the arbitrator's decision within a certain number days after the decision is rendered. Under most state laws, if you are dissatisfied with the arbitrator's decision, you can go to court and sue for a replacement car or a refund.

THE FLORIDA LEMON LAW DISPUTE SETTLEMENT PROCEDURES

Florida has a comprehensive lemon law statute which includes a detailed dispute settlement procedure, as follows.

Florida State Statutes

Chapter 681

Motor Vehicle Sales Warranties

Motor Vehicle Warranty Enforcement Act

681.108 Dispute-settlement procedures.

(1) If a manufacturer has established a procedure—and has informed the consumer how and where to file a claim with such procedure—the provisions [herein] apply to the consumer only if the consumer has first resorted to such procedure. The decision makers for a certified procedure shall, in rendering decisions, take into account all legal and equitable factors germane to a fair and just decision, including, but not limited to, the warranty; the rights and remedies conferred under the provisions of this chapter; and any other equitable considerations appropriate under the circumstances. Decision makers and staff of a procedure shall be trained in the provisions of this chapter. In an action brought by a consumer concerning an alleged nonconformity, the decision that results from a certified procedure is admissible in evidence.

(2) A manufacturer may apply to the division for certification of its procedure. After receipt and evaluation of the application, the division shall certify the procedure or notify the manufacturer of any deficiencies in the application or the procedure.

(3) A certified procedure or a procedure of an applicant seeking certification shall submit to the division a copy of each settlement approved by the procedure or decision made by a decision maker within 30 days

after the settlement is reached or the decision is rendered. The decision or settlement must contain at a minimum the:

1. Name and address of the consumer;

2. Name of the manufacturer and address of the dealership from which the motor vehicle was purchased;

3. Date the claim was received and the location of the procedure office that handled the claim;

4. Relief requested by the consumer;

5. Name of each decision maker rendering the decision or person approving the settlement;

6. Statement of the terms of the settlement or decision;

7. Date of the settlement or decision; and

8. Statement of whether the decision was accepted or rejected by the consumer.

(4) Any manufacturer establishing or applying to establish a certified procedure must file with the division a copy of the annual report, together with any additional information required for purposes of certification, including the number of refunds and replacements made in this state pursuant to the provisions of this chapter by the manufacturer during the period audited.

(5) The division shall review each certified procedure at least annually, prepare an annual report evaluating the operation of certified procedures established by motor vehicle manufacturers and procedures of applicants seeking certification, and, for a period not to exceed 1 year, shall grant certification to, or renew certification for, those manufacturers whose procedures substantially comply with the provisions of this chapter and rules adopted under this chapter. If certification is revoked or denied, the division shall state the reasons for such action. The reports and records of actions taken with respect to certification shall be public records.

(6) A manufacturer whose certification is denied or revoked is entitled to a hearing.

(7) If federal preemption of state authority to regulate procedures occurs, the provisions of subsection (1) concerning prior resort do not apply.

(8) The division shall adopt rules to implement this section.

681.109 Florida New Motor Vehicle Arbitration Board.

Dispute Eligibility.

(1) If a manufacturer has a certified procedure, a consumer claim arising during the Lemon Law rights period must be filed with the certified procedure no later than 60 days after the expiration of the Lemon Law rights period. If a decision is not rendered by the certified procedure within 40 days of filing, the consumer may apply to the division to have the dispute removed to the board for arbitration.

(2) If a manufacturer has a certified procedure, a consumer claim arising during the Lemon Law rights period must be filed with the certified procedure no later than 60 days after the expiration of the Lemon Law rights period. If a consumer is not satisfied with the decision or the manufacturer's compliance therewith, the consumer may apply to the division to have the dispute submitted to the board for arbitration. A manufacturer may not seek review of a decision made under its procedure.

(3) If a manufacturer has no certified procedure or if a certified procedure does not have jurisdiction to resolve the dispute, a consumer may apply directly to the division to have the dispute submitted to the board for arbitration.

(4) A consumer must request arbitration before the board with respect to a claim arising during the Lemon Law rights period no later than 60 days after the expiration of the Lemon Law rights period, or within 30 days after the final action of a certified procedure, whichever date occurs later.

(5) The division shall screen all requests for arbitration before the board to determine eligibility. The consumer's request for arbitration before the board shall be made on a form prescribed by the department. The division shall forward to the board all disputes that the division determines are potentially entitled to relief under this chapter.

(6) The division may reject a dispute that it determines to be fraudulent or outside the scope of the board's authority. Any dispute deemed by the division to be ineligible for arbitration by the board due to insufficient evidence may be reconsidered upon the submission of new information regarding the dispute. Following a second review, the division may reject a dispute if the evidence is clearly insufficient to qualify for relief. Any dispute rejected by the division shall be forwarded to the department and a copy shall be sent by registered mail to the consumer and the manufacturer, containing a brief explanation as to the reason for rejection.

(7) If the division rejects a dispute, the consumer may file a lawsuit to enforce the remedies provided under this chapter. In any civil action arising under this chapter and relating to a matter considered by the division, any determination made to reject a dispute is admissible in evidence.

(8) The department shall have the authority to adopt reasonable rules to carry out the provisions of this section.

681.1095 Florida New Motor Vehicle Arbitration Board.

Creation and Function.

(1) There is established within the Department of Legal Affairs, the Florida New Motor Vehicle Arbitration Board, consisting of members appointed by the Attorney General for an initial term of 1 year. Board members may be reappointed for additional terms of 2 years. Each board member is accountable to the Attorney General for the performance of the member's duties and is exempt from civil liability for any act or omission that occurs while acting in the member's official capacity. The Department of Legal Affairs shall defend a member in any action against the member or the board that arises from any such act or omission. The Attorney General may establish as many regions of the board as necessary to carry out the provisions of this chapter.

(2) The boards shall hear cases in various locations throughout the state so any consumer whose dispute is approved for arbitration by the division may attend an arbitration hearing at a reasonably convenient location and present a dispute orally. Hearings shall be conducted by panels of three board members assigned by the department. A majority vote of the three-member board panel shall be required to render a decision. Arbitration proceedings under this section shall be open to the public on reasonable and nondiscriminatory terms.

(3) Each region of the board shall consist of up to eight members. The members of the board shall construe and apply the provisions of this chapter, and rules adopted thereunder, in making their decisions. An administrator and a secretary shall be assigned to each board by the Department of Legal Affairs. At least one member of each board must be a person with expertise in motor vehicle mechanics. A member must not be employed by a manufacturer or a franchised motor vehicle dealer or be a staff member, a decision maker, or a consultant for a procedure. Board members shall be trained in the application of this chapter and any rules adopted under this chapter, shall be reimbursed for travel expenses and shall be compensated at a rate or wage prescribed by the Attorney General.

(4) Before filing a civil action, the consumer must first submit the dispute to the division, and to the board if such dispute is deemed eligible for arbitration.

(5) Manufacturers shall submit to arbitration conducted by the board if such arbitration is requested by a consumer and the dispute is deemed eligible for arbitration by the division.

(6) The board shall hear the dispute within 40 days and render a decision within 60 days after the date the request for arbitration is approved. The board may continue the hearing on its own motion or upon the request of a party for good cause shown. A request for continuance by the consumer constitutes waiver of the time periods set forth in this subsection. The Department of Legal Affairs, at the board's request, may investigate disputes, and may issue subpoenas for the attendance of witnesses and for the production of records, documents, and other evidence before the board. The failure of the board to hear a dispute or render a decision within the prescribed periods does not invalidate the decision.

(7) At all arbitration proceedings, the parties may present oral and written testimony, present witnesses and evidence relevant to the dispute, cross-examine witnesses, and be represented by counsel. The board may administer oaths or affirmations to witnesses and inspect the vehicle if requested by a party or if the board deems such inspection appropriate.

(8) The board shall grant relief, if a reasonable number of attempts have been undertaken to correct nonconformity or nonconformities.

(9) The decision of the board shall be sent by registered mail to the consumer and the manufacturer, and shall contain written findings of fact and rationale for the decision. If the decision is in favor of the consumer, the manufacturer must, within 40 days after receipt of the decision, comply with the terms of the decision. Compliance occurs on the date the consumer receives delivery of an acceptable replacement motor vehicle or the refund specified in the arbitration award. In any civil action arising under this chapter and relating to a dispute arbitrated before the board, any decision by the board is admissible in evidence.

(10) A decision is final unless appealed by either party. A petition to the circuit court to appeal a decision must be made within 30 days after receipt of the decision. The petition shall be filed in the county where the consumer resides, or where the motor vehicle was acquired, or where the arbitration hearing was conducted. Within 7 days after the petition has been filed, the appealing party must send a copy of the petition to the department. If the department does not receive notice of such petition within 40 days after the manufacturer's receipt of a deci-

sion in favor of the consumer, and the manufacturer has neither complied with, nor has petitioned to appeal such decision, the department may apply to the circuit court to seek imposition of a fine up to $1,000 per day against the manufacturer until the amount stands at twice the purchase price of the motor vehicle, unless the manufacturer provides clear and convincing evidence that the delay or failure was beyond its control or was acceptable to the consumer as evidenced by a written statement signed by the consumer. If the manufacturer fails to provide such evidence or fails to pay the fine, the department shall initiate proceedings against the manufacturer for failure to pay such fine. The proceeds from the fine herein imposed shall be placed in the Motor Vehicle Warranty Trust Fund in the department for implementation and enforcement of this chapter. If the manufacturer fails to comply with the provisions of this subsection, the court shall affirm the award upon application by the consumer.

(11) All provisions pertaining to compulsory arbitration before the board, the dispute eligibility screening by the division, the proceedings and decisions of the board, and any appeals thereof, are exempt from the provisions of chapter 120.

(12) An appeal of a decision by the board to the circuit court by a consumer or a manufacturer shall be by trial de novo. In a written petition to appeal a decision by the board, the appealing party must state the action requested and the grounds relied upon for appeal. Within 30 days of final disposition of the appeal, the appealing party shall furnish the department with notice of such disposition and, upon request, shall furnish the department with a copy of the order or judgment of the court.

(13) If a decision of the board in favor of the consumer is upheld by the court, recovery by the consumer shall include the pecuniary value of the award, attorney's fees incurred in obtaining confirmation of the award, and all costs and continuing damages in the amount of $25 per day for each day beyond the 40-day period following the manufacturer's receipt of the board's decision. If a court determines that the manufacturer acted in bad faith in bringing the appeal or brought the appeal solely for the purpose of harassment or in complete absence of a justiciable issue of law or fact, the court shall double, and may triple, the amount of the total award.

(14) When a judgment affirms a decision by the board in favor of a consumer, appellate review may be conditioned upon payment by the manufacturer of the consumer's attorney's fees and giving security for costs and expenses resulting from the review period.

(15) The department shall maintain records of each dispute submitted to the board, and the program, including an index of motor vehicles by year, make, and model, and shall compile aggregate annual statistics for all disputes submitted to, and decided by, the board, as well as annual statistics for each manufacturer that include, but are not limited to, the value, if applicable, and the number and percent of:

(a) Replacement motor vehicle requests;

(b) Purchase price refund requests;

(c) Replacement motor vehicles obtained in prehearing settlements;

(d) Purchase price refunds obtained in prehearing settlements;

(e) Replacement motor vehicles awarded in arbitration;

(f) Purchase price refunds awarded in arbitration;

(g) Board decisions neither complied with in 40 days nor petitioned for appeal within 30 days;

(h) Board decisions appealed;

(i) Appeals affirmed by the court; and

(j) Appeals found by the court to be brought in bad faith or solely for the purpose of harassment.

The statistics compiled under this subsection are public information.

(16) When requested by the department, a manufacturer must verify the settlement terms for disputes that are approved for arbitration but are not decided by the board.

GOING TO COURT

If there is no state-certified arbitration program, or if the state's law gives you the right to go directly to court, you can file a lawsuit against the manufacturer. You can also go to court if you are dissatisfied with the arbitrator's decision, provided the decision was not binding. If you go to court, you should hire an attorney to assist you, as litigation is more formal and more complex than arbitration. The attorney should be experienced with the state's lemon law and consumer warranty law, and should be one who routinely represents consumers and not automobile manufacturers. If you prevail in court, you may be able to recover a greater refund, including costs and attorney fees.

CHAPTER 5:
SAFETY STANDARDS AND RECALLS

VEHICLE SAFETY STANDARDS

Pursuant to the National Traffic and Motor Vehicle Safety Act, the National Highway Traffic and Safety Administration (NHTSA) is authorized to issue vehicle safety standards and require manufacturers to recall vehicles with safety-related defects. These federal safety standards apply to all vehicles and equipment manufactured or imported for sale in the United States, which will be used on public roads and highways.

The safety standards set minimum performance requirements for those parts of a vehicle that protect the drivers and passengers from death or serious injury in the event of an accident. This includes the air bags, seat belts, steering column, etc. If a car does not comply with one of the vehicle safety standards, it is subject to recall.

SAFETY-RELATED DEFECTS

According to the NHTSA, a safety-related defect is a problem that exists in a motor vehicle or item of motor vehicle equipment that:

1. Poses a risk to motor vehicle safety, and

2. May exist in a group of vehicles of the same design or manufacture, or items of equipment of the same type and manufacture.

Safety defects would not include problems with the air conditioning, radio, paint, or ordinary wear of equipment that must be periodically replaced, such as batteries, brake pads, etc. Safety defects are usually the result of inadequate design or manufacturing error, and may include:

1. Steering components that break suddenly causing partial or complete loss of vehicle control.

2. Problems with fuel system components, particularly in their susceptibility to crash damage, that result in leakage of fuel and possibly cause vehicle fires.

3. Accelerator controls that may break or stick.

4. Wheels that crack or break, resulting in loss of vehicle control.

5. Engine cooling fan blades that break unexpectedly causing injury to persons working on a vehicle.

6. Windshield wiper assemblies that fail to operate or malfunction.

7. Seats and/or seat backs that fail unexpectedly during normal use.

8. Critical vehicle components that break, fall apart, or separate from the vehicle causing loss of vehicle control or injury to persons inside or outside the vehicle.

9. Wiring system problems that result in a fire or loss of lighting.

10. Car ramps or jacks that collapse causing injury to someone working on a vehicle.

11. Air bags that deploy under conditions for which they are not designed to deploy.

12. Child safety seats that contain defective safety belts, buckles, or components that create a risk of injury, not only in a vehicle crash but also in non-operational safety of a motor vehicle.

If a safety defect is discovered, the manufacturer must notify the NHTSA, distributors, dealerships, and vehicle owners. The NHTSA will then monitor the manufacturer's corrective action and make sure they comply with the statutory safety standards.

REPORTING A SAFETY DEFECT

If you think your car has a safety defect, you should report it to the NHTSA. The NHTSA maintains a list of these reports and, if they receive a substantial number of similar complaints, they will initiate an investigation. You can file a complaint by mail, telephone or internet, as follows:

United States Department of Transportation
National Highway Traffic and Safety Administration
Office of Defects Investigation
400 7th Street, S.W.
Washington, DC 20590
Auto Safety Hotline: 1-888-327-4236
Website: www.nhtsa.dot.gov

The NHTSA operates a hotline in order to collect complaints about vehicle safety problems. When you call the hotline, you will be required to provide certain information so NHTSA staff can evaluate your car's problem. The information is entered into the consumer complaint database and a record of the report called a Vehicle Owner's Questionnaire (VOQ) is generated and given to the technical staff to evaluate. The VOQ is also mailed to you so you can verify the information and provide additional details, if any. If the problem you reported is already under investigation, your report will be added to the investigation file.

THE NHTSA INVESTIGATION PROCEDURE

All of the complaints entered into the consumer complaint database, including VOQs, letters, emails, etc., are given to the NHTSA Office of Defects Investigation (ODI).

Based on a review of the filed reports, the NHTSA and the manufacturers decide whether a safety recall is warranted. The number of complaints and severity of consequences are measured against the number of cars and how many years the cars have been in service. If a trend is suspected suggesting a safety risk, the NHTSA will conduct a more detailed analysis and investigation of the problem.

The NHTSA investigation procedure includes:

Screening

The ODI conducts a preliminary review of all of the consumer complaints entered into the database to decide whether an investigation is warranted. You can access the consumer complaint database on the internet at: www.nhtsa.dot.gov/cars/problems. The database is updated weekly, and includes a copy of each complaint reported to the NHTSA.

Petition Analysis

The NHTSA also process petitions for defect investigations and safety recall problems. Any person is permitted to petition the NHTSA to start an investigation into an alleged safety defect. The ODI will inform the petitioner whether the petition has been granted or denied. If granted, a defect investigation is opened. If the petition is denied, the reasons are published in the Federal Register.

Investigation

Investigations are conducted in two phases:

Preliminary Evaluation

Most preliminary evaluations are based on information received. The ODI obtains certain information from the manufacturer, including data on complaints, crashes, injuries, warranty claims, and modifications. The manufacturer is permitted to present its views regarding the alleged defect. Preliminary evaluations take approximately four months to complete. They are either closed on the basis that further investigation is not necessary, or because the manufacturer has decided to issue a recall. If the ODI believes further investigation is warranted, they conduct a more detailed investigation known as an engineering analysis.

Engineering Analysis

During an engineering analysis, the ODI conducts a more detailed and complete analysis of the alleged defect, including inspections, tests, and surveys. The ODI also collects additional information from the manufacturer, The engineering analysis takes approximately one year to complete at which time the investigation may be closed if the agency is unable to identify the safety defect, or if the manufacturer conducts a safety recall either voluntarily or in response to NHTSA recall request letter.

Recall Management

Recall management involves an investigation of the adequacy of the manufacturer's safety recalls. The NHTSA's Recall Mangement Division (RMD) maintains records of all safety recalls, and monitors the recalls to make sure that they are carried out properly.

The manufacturer can challenge the NHTSA's recall order and determination that a safety-related defect exists in a Federal District Court. The agency can also go to court to compel the manufacturer to comply with the recall order. While the case is pending, however, the manufacturer may be required to notify consumers of the NHTSA's order, and the manufacturer's challenge to the NHTSA order.

Nevertheless, most recalls are made by manufacturers voluntarily after testing and inspection before NHTSA involvement. The manufacturer is then required to report its findings to the NHTSA and fix the problem.

CONSUMER NOTIFICATION

Manufacturers are required to notify registered owners and purchasers of affected vehicles within a reasonable time after a safety defect determination is made. Notice must be given by first-class mail with an explanation of the safety defect and potential risks. The notice must advise consumers how and where to get the problem fixed at no cost to the consumer, and how long it will take to repair the problem.

If you believe your car may be involved in a recall, but you have not received a notice from the manufacturer, you can contact the NHTSA by telephone or visit their website listed above, contact the manufacturer, or contact the dealer where you purchased your car.

REMEDIES

After a determination has been made that a particular vehicle has a safety-related defect, the manufacturer has three options for correcting the defect: (1) repair the defect; (2) replace the vehicle with an identical or similar vehicle; or (3) refund the purchase price of the vehicle.

If you have the repair performed prior to the manufacturer's recall, you may be entitled to reimbursement of your repair costs. However, manufacturers are only obligated to provide a remedy at no cost to the consumer if the vehicle is no more than 10 years old on the date the defect is determined to exist. Further, if a court determines that the NHTSA's determination was incorrect, the manufacturer will not be obligated to reimburse you for your repair costs.

If the dealer refuses to repair your vehicle at no charge following a recall notice, and you are entitled to this remedy under the law, you should contact the manufacturer immediately. Most dealers have contractual obligations to the manufacturer to honor recall notices and repair safety defects at no cost to the consumer.

CHAPTER 6:
MAKING AN INFORMED CAR PURCHASE

IN GENERAL

This almanac discusses your rights under the law if you buy a car that turns out to be a lemon. As the saying goes, "an ounce of prevention is worth a pound of cure." This chapter provides information that will help you make an informed purchase to decrease the odds of your getting stuck with a lemon car.

NEW AUTOMOBILE PURCHASES

A new car is a large-ticket item which must be thoroughly researched before purchasing. Don't rush into a new car purchase before checking with consumer publications concerning the vehicle's ratings for safety, quality, and cost comparison, etc. Make sure you carefully read every document you are asked to sign. Most new cars come with some kind of warranty. Make sure you carefully read your warranty and know what is covered and what is not covered. If you don't understand certain terms, get professional advice. Don't rely on the salesperson's representations. The salesperson's primary interest is to sell you the car. Don't be pressured into making a deal you will regret with costly consequences later.

Keep copies of the documents about your car, including warranties, advertisements, and brochures in case the car fails to conform. Inspect your new car before you accept delivery. If you detect any problems, refuse delivery until the problem has been fixed. Don't accept delivery and hope the problem can be fixed later.

USED AUTOMOBILE PURCHASES

Before shopping for a used vehicle, you should check out used car guides, newspaper ads and classifieds to get an idea of a fair price range for the particular car you are seeking. Contact the Auto Safety

Hotline at (800) 424-9393 for recall information on the type of car you intend to purchase.

Before purchasing the car, make sure you take a test drive. Bring your own mechanic with you so he or she can inspect the vehicle. You are entitled to information concerning previous ownership of the car, including its mechanical history, and whether it has been involved in any accidents. Obtain the car's vehicle identification number (VIN) so you can obtain an independent vehicle history report.

Make sure that you carefully read the purchase agreement prior to signing to ensure that it accurately reflects the details of the transaction. If you were promised something that is not written in the agreement, make sure that it is included before you sign. Inquire about the warranty provisions of the car and make sure you get them in writing. Used cars may still be under the manufacturer's original warranty, or you may be able to purchase an extended warranty. Make sure you carefully read your warranty and know what is covered and what is not covered. Also, ask to see the maintenance and service records for the car, if available.

Some unscrupulous used car dealers fail to register the car in the dealer name to avoid being subject to the law. Instead, they maintain the registration in the previous owner's name and make the deal as if you were buying the car from the private individual. Make sure you check the vehicle registration and title to ensure that the seller is the registered owner of the vehicle.

VEHICLE TITLE WASHING

Vehicle title washing refers to vehicles that have been severely damaged in one state, and then rebuilt and sold in another state where a new title is obtained and the purchaser has no idea that the car was once a wreck. These cars are likely to break down and cause the unwary purchaser a lot of repair costs not to mention the safety concerns.

A minority of states, including California, Michigan, and Iowa, have consumer protection laws that prohibit the retitling of a vehicle that has been totaled and is unrepairable. Many states do not have such protection, and vehicles are often moved into those states, retitled and sold to unsuspecting buyers.

There is federal legislation pending that would provide a uniform national standard for handling wrecked and salvaged vehicles, and that would require warning labels on rebuilt salvage cars—e.g., cars that sustained damage exceeding a certain percentage of the car's pre-accident value. The law would also require owners of wrecked and salvaged vehicles to disclose any damage exceeding a certain dollar amount.

It may be difficult to spot a car that has been title washed. If the car has an out-of-state title, check to see if the title indicates whether the car has been salvaged. If not, you can try and inspect the car to see whether it has had any damage, e.g., mismatched paint; misaligned hood or trunk, etc. Have a mechanic inspect the underbody of the vehicle to see whether the frame has been bent. Check for rust in the interior that may indicate water damage.

APPENDIX 1:
STATE LEMON LAW STATUTE CITATIONS

STATE	STATUTE	TITLE
Alabama	Alabama State Statutes, Title 8, Section 20A	Commercial Law And Consumer Protection, Motor Vehicle Lemon Law Rights
Alaska	Alaska State Statutes, Title 45, Chapter 45	Trade And Commerce, Trade Practices
Arizona	Arizona State Statutes, Title 44, Article 5	Trade And Commerce, Motor Vehicle Warranties
Arkansas	Arkansas State Statutes, Title 4, Subtitle 7, Chapter 90, Subchapter 4	Arkansas New Motor Vehicle Quality Assurance Act
California	California State Statutes, Civil Code Section 1793.22-1793.26	Sale Warranties, Tanner Consumer Protection Act, Used Car Disclosures
Colorado	Colorado State Statutes, Statutes 42-10-101	n/a
Connecticut	Connecticut State Statutes, Title-42, Chapter 743b	Business, Selling, Trading and Collection Practices, New Automobile Warranties
Delaware	Delaware State Statutes, Title 6, Subtitle II, Chapter 50, Sections 5001-5009	Commerce And Trade, Automobile Warranties
Florida	Florida State Statutes, Chapter 681	Motor Vehicle Sales Warranties, Motor Vehicle Warranty Enforcement Act
Georgia	Georgia State Statutes, Section 10-1-780–10-1-792	Motor Vehicle Warranty Rights Act
Hawaii	Hawaii State Statutes, Title 26, Chapter 481I	Trade Regulation And Practice, Motor Vehicle Express Warranty Enforcement

STATE	STATUTE	TITLE
Idaho	Idaho State Statutes, Title 48, Chapter 9, Sections 901-913	Monopolies And Trade Practices, New Motor Vehicle Warranties, Manufacturer's Duty to Repair, Refund or Replace
Illinois	Illinois State Statutes, Chapter 815, Section 380	Business Transactions, New Vehicle Buyer Protection Act
Indiana	Indiana State Statutes, Title 24, Article 5, Chapter 13	Trade Regulations; Consumer Sales And Credit, Motor Vehicle Protection, Buyback Vehicle Disclosure
Iowa	Iowa State Statutes, Chapter 322G	n/a
Kansas	Kansas State Statutes, Chapter 50, Article 6	Unfair Trade and Consumer Protection
Kentucky	Kentucky State Statutes, Chapter 367, Section 840	Consumer Protection
Louisiana	n/a	n/a
Maine	Maine State Statutes, Title 10, Chapter 203-A	Warranties On New Motor Vehicles
Maryland	Maryland State Statues, Annotated Code of Maryland, §§ 14-1501–14-1504	Commercial Law, Automotive Warranty Enforcement Act
Massachusetts	Massachusetts State Statutes, Chapter 90, Section 7N	Voiding Contracts Of Sale
Michigan	Michigan State Statutes, MCL 257.1401– MCL 257.1410	New Motor Vehicle Warranties
Minnesota	Minnesota State Statutes, Chapter 325F, Section 665	Trade Regulations, Consumer Protection, Products And Sales
Mississippi	Mississippi State Statutes, Title 63, Chapter 17, Sections 151-165	Motor Vehicle Warranty Enforcement Act
Missouri	Missouri State Statutes, Title XXVI, Chapter 407, Sections 560-583	n/a
Montana	Montana State Statutes, Title 61, Chapter 4, Part 5	New Motor Vehicle Warranties—Remedies

STATE	STATUTE	TITLE
Nebraska	Nebraska State Statutes, Chapter 60, Sections 2701-2709	Motor Vehicles
Nevada	Nevada State Statutes, NRS 597.600 to 597.690	Repairs To Conform To Express Warranties
New Hampshire	New Hampshire State Statutes, Title 31—Chapter 357D	Trade and Commerce, New Motor Vehicle Arbitration
New Jersey	New Jersey State Statutes, 56:12-29–56:12-49	Unfair Trade Practices
New Mexico	New Mexico State Statutes, Chapter 57, Article 16A	Motor Vehicle Quality Assurance Act
New York	New York State Statutes, Article 11-A, Section 198	General Business, Motor Vehicle Manufacturers
North Carolina	North Carolina State Statutes, Article 15A, Chapter 20, Section 351	New Motor Vehicles Warranties Act
North Dakota	North Dakota State Statutes, Chapter 51-07, Sections 16-22	Sales And Exchanges, Miscellaneous Provisions
Ohio	Ohio State Statutes, Sections 1345.71–1345.77	Nonconforming New Motor Vehicles
Oklahoma	Oklahoma State Statutes, Title 15, Chapter 22, Section 901	Contracts
Oregon	Oregon State Statutes, ORS 646.315–646.375	Trade Practices and Antitrust Regulation, Enforcement Of Express Warranties On New Motor Vehicles
Pennsylvania	Pennsylvania State Statutes, Title 73, Chapter 28	Trade And Commerce, Automobile Lemon Law
Rhode Island	Rhode Island State Statutes, Chapter 31-5.2	Motor And Other Vehicles, Consumer Enforcement of Motor Vehicle Warranties
South Carolina	South Carolina State Statutes, Title 56, Chapter 28	Enforcement Of Motor Vehicle Express Warranties
South Dakota	South Dakota State Statutes, Title 32, Chapter 6D	Manufacturer's Warranty
Tennessee	Tennessee State Statutes, Title 55, Chapter 24	Motor Vehicle Warranties

STATE	STATUTE	TITLE
Texas	Texas State Statutes, Sections 3.08i, 6.07, 7.01, 107.1-107.12	Texas Motor Vehicle Commission, Warranty Performance Obligations
Utah	Utah State Statutes, Title 13, Chapter 20	New Motor Vehicle Warranties Act
Vermont	Vermont State Statutes, Title 9, Chapter 115, Sections 4170-4181	Commerce and Trade, New Motor Vehicle Arbitration
Virginia	Virginia State Statutes, Title 59.1, Chapter 17.3	Trade And Commerce, Virginia Motor Vehicle Warranty Enforcement Act
Washington	Washington State Statutes, Title 19, Chapter 118	Motor Vehicle Warranties
West Virginia	West Virginia State Statutes, Chapter 46A, Article 6A	Consumer Protection, New Motor Vehicle Warranties
Wisconsin	Wisconsin State Statutes, Chapter 218, Subchapter I	Motor Vehicle Dealers, Repair, Replacement and Refund
Wyoming	Wyoming State Statutes, Title 40, Chapter 17, Section 101	Motor Vehicles

APPENDIX 2:
STATE LEMON LAW WEBSITES

STATE	WEBSITE
Alabama	http://www.ago.alabama.gov/alcode/law_lemon.htm
Alaska	http://www.law.state.ak.us/department/civil/consumer/cpindex.html
Arizona	http://www.azag.gov/consumer/index.html
Arkansas	http://www.ag.state.ar.us/consumer/lemonlaw.html
California	http://caag.state.ca.us/consumers/general/lemon.htm
Colorado	http://www.ago.state.co.us/consprot/lemonlaw/Lemonlaw.htm
Connecticut	http://www.ct.gov/dcp/site/default.asp
Delaware	http://www.ct.gov/dcp/site/default.asp
District of Columbia	http://occ.dc.gov/occ/cwp/view.asp?a=1223&q=531275
Florida	http://occ.dc.gov/occ/cwp/view.asp?a=1223&q=531275
Georgia	http://consumer.georgia.gov
Hawaii	http://www.hawaii.gov/dcca/areas/rico
Idaho	http://www2.state.id.us/ag/consumer/index.htm
Illinois	http://www.ag.state.il.us/consumers/index.html
Indiana	http://www.in.gov/attorneygeneral/consumer/lemonlaw.html
Iowa	http://www.state.ia.us/government/ag/consumer/advisories/lemonlawall020402.html
Kansas	http://www.ksag.org/Publications/ConsumerCorner/Car/index.htm
Kentucky	http://www.law.state.ky.us/cp/cptips.htm#New%20Cars
Louisiana	http://ladoj.ag.state.la.us/publications/lemonlaw2.htm
Maine	http://www.maine.gov/ag/index.php?r=protection&s=lemon_law&t=
Maryland	http://www.oag.state.md.us/consumer/lemon.htm

STATE	WEBSITE
Massachusetts	http://www.mass.gov/poral/site/massgovportal/menuitem.91646817bed931c14db4a11030468a0c/?pageID=ocasubtopic&L=4&sid=Eoca&L0=Home&L1=Consumer&L2=Autos&L3=Buying+and+Selling
Michigan	http://www.michigan.gov/ag/0,1607,7-164-17331-42077—,00.html
Minnesota	http://www.ag.state.mn.us/consumer/cars/MNCarlaws/MNCarLaws_1.htm
Mississippi	http://www.ago.state.ms.us/divisions/consumer/
Missouri	http://www.ago.state.mo.us/consumercomplaint.htm
Montana	http://www.discoveringmontana.com/doa/consumer protection/lemonlaw.asp
Nebraska	http://www.dmv.state.ne.us/legal/lemon.html
Nevada	http://ag.state.nv.us/actionbutton/bcp/bcp.htm
New Hampshire	http://nh.gov/safety/dmv/lemonlaw/index.html
New Jersey	http://www.state.nj.us/lps/ca/brief/lemon.htm
New Mexico	http://www.ago.state.nm.us/divs/cons/cons_faqs_auto.htm
New York	http://www.oag.state.ny.us/consumer/cars/newcarlemon.html
North Carolina	http://www.jus.state.nc.us/cp/lemon.htm
North Dakota	http://www.ag.state.nd.us
Ohio	http://www.ag.state.oh.us/index.asp
Oklahoma	http://www.oag.state.ok.us/
Oregon	http://www.doj.state.or.us/lemonlaw.htm
Pennsylvania	http://www.attorneygeneral.gov/pei/know/lemonlaw.htm
Rhode Island	http://www.riag.state.ri.us/civil/index.php
South Carolina	http://www.scconsumer.gov/
South Dakota	http://www.state.sd.us/attorney/office/divisions/consumer/default.asp
Tennessee	http://www.state.tn.us/consumer/lemon.html
Texas	http://www.dot.state.tx.us/mvd/lemon/lemonlaw.htm
Utah	http://www.commerce.utah.gov/dcp/education/lemonlaw.html
Vermont	http://www.aot.state.vt.us/dmv/LAWS/LEMONLAW/LAWSLemon.htm
Virginia	http://www.vdacs.virginia.gov/consumers/oca.html
Washington	http://www.atg.wa.gov/consumer/lemon/
West Virginia	http://www.wvs.state.wv.us/wvag/

STATE	WEBSITE
Wisconsin	http://www.dot.wisconsin.gov/safety/consumer/rights/ lemonlaw.htm
Wyoming	http://attorneygeneral.state.wy.us/consumer.htm

APPENDIX 3:
DIRECTORY OF STATE ATTORNEY GENERAL OFFICES

STATE	TELEPHONE	ADDRESS	WEBSITE
Alabama	334-242-7300	State House 11 S. Union St. Montgomery, AL 36130	http://www.ago.state.al.us
Alaska	907-465-3600	P.O. Box 110300 Diamond Courthouse Juneau, AK 99811-0300	http://www.law.state.ak.us
Arizona	602-542-4266	1275 W. Washington St. Phoenix, AZ 85007	http://www.attorneygeneral.state.az.us
Arkansas	800-482-8982	200 Tower Bldg. 323 Center St. Little Rock, AR 72201-2610	http://www.ag.state.ar.us

STATE	TELEPHONE	ADDRESS	WEBSITE
California	916-445-9555	1300 I St. Ste. 1740 Sacramento, CA 95814	http://caag.state.ca.us
Colorado	303-866-4500	Dept. of Law 1525 Sherman St. Denver, CO 80203	http://www.ago.state.co.us
Connecticut	860-808-5318	55 Elm St. Hartford, CT 06141-0120	http://www.cslib.org/attygenl/
Delaware	302-577-8338	Carvel State , Office Bldg. 820 N. French St. Wilmington, DE 19801	http://www.state.de.us/attgen
District of Columbia	202-724-1305	Office of the Corporation Counsel 441 4th St. NW, Washington, DC 20001	http://occ.dc.gov
Florida	850-487-1963	The Capitol, PL 01 Tallahassee, FL 32399-1050	http://myfloridalegal.com/
Georgia	404-656-3300	40 Capitol Square, SW Atlanta, GA 30334-1300	http://ganet.org/ago/
Hawaii	808-586-1500	425 Queen St. Honolulu, HI 96813	http://www.state.hi.us/ag/index.html
Idaho	208-334-2400	Statehouse Boise, ID 83720-1000	http://www2.state.id.us/ag/
Illinois	312-814-3000	James R. Thompson Ctr. 100 W. Randolph St. Chicago, IL 60601	http://www.ag.state.il.us

STATE	TELEPHONE	ADDRESS	WEBSITE
Indiana	317-232-6201	Indiana Government Center South- 5th Floor 402 West Washington Street Indianapolis, IN 46204	http://www.in.gov/attorneygeneral/
Iowa	515-281-5164	Hoover State , Office Bldg. 1305 E. Walnut Des Moines, IA 50319	http://www.IowaAttorneyGeneral.org
Kansas	785-296-2215	120 S.W. 10th Ave., 2nd Fl. Topeka, KS 66612-1597	http://www.ink.org/public/ksag
Kentucky	502-696-5300	State Capitol, Rm. 116 Frankfort, KY 40601	http://www.law.state.ky.us
Louisiana	225-342-7013	Dept. of Justice P.O. Box 94095, Baton Rouge, LA 70804-4095	http://www.ag.state.la.us/
Maine	207-626-8800	State House Station 6 Augusta, ME 04333	http://www.state.me.us/ag
Maryland	410-576-6300	200 St., Paul Place Baltimore, MD 21202-2202	http://www.oag.state.ma.us
Massachusetts	617-727-2200	1 Ashburton Place Boston, MA 02108-1698	http://www.ago.state.ma.us
Michigan	517-373-1110	P.O. Box 30212 525 W. Ottawa St. Lansing, MI 48909-0212	http://www.ag.state.mi.us
Minnesota	651-296-3353	State Capitol, Ste. 102 St. Paul, MN 55155	http://www.ag.state.mn.us

STATE	TELEPHONE	ADDRESS	WEBSITE
Mississippi	601-359-3680	Dept. of Justice P.O. Box 220, Jackson MS 39205-0220	http://www.ago.state.ms.us
Missouri	573-751-3321	Supreme Ct. Bldg. 207 W. High St. Jefferson City, MO 65101	http://www.ago.state.mo.us
Montana	406-444-2026	Justice Bldg. 215 N. Sanders Helena, MT 59620-1401	http://doj.state.mt.us/
Nebraska	402-471-2682	State Capitol P.O. Box 98920 Lincoln, NE 68509-8920	http://www.nol.org/home/ago
Nevada	775-684-1100	Old Supreme, Ct. Bldg. 100 N. Carson St. Carson City, NV 89701	http://ag.state.nv.us/
New Hampshire	603-271-3658	33 Capitol Street Concord, NH 03301-6397	http://www.state.nh.us/nhdoj
New Jersey	609-292-8740	Richard J. Hughes Justice Complex 25 Market St. CN 080, Trenton, NJ 08625	http://www.state.nj.us/lps/
New Mexico	505-827-6000	P.O. Drawer 1508 Sante Fe, NM 87504-1508	http://www.ago.state.nm.us
New York	518-474-7330	Dept. of Law- The Capitol, 2nd Fl. Albany, NY 12224	http://www.oag.state.ny.us

STATE	TELEPHONE	ADDRESS	WEBSITE
North Carolina	919-716-6400	Dept. of Justice P.O. Box 629 Raleigh, NC 27602-0629	http://www.jus.state.nc.us
North Dakota	701-328-2210	State Capitol 600 E. Boulevard Ave. Bismarck, ND 58505-0040	http://www.ag.state.nd.us
Ohio	614-466-4320	State Office Tower 30 E. Broad St. Columbus, OH 43266-0410	http://www.ag.state.oh.us
Oklahoma	405-521-3921	State Capitol, Rm. 112 2300 N. Lincoln Blvd. Oklahoma City, OK 73105	http://www.oag.state.ok.us
Oregon	503-378-4732	Justice Bldg. 1162 Court St. NE, Salem, OR 97301	http://www.doj.state.or.us
Pennsylvania	717-787-3391	Strawberry Square Harrisburg, PA 17120	http://www.attorneygeneral.gov
Rhode Island	401-274-4400	150 S. Main St. Providence, RI 02903	http://www.riag.state.ri.us
South Carolina	803-734-4399	Rembert C. Dennis Office Bldg. P.O. Box 11549 Columbia, SC 29211-1549	http://www.scattorneygeneral.org
South Dakota	605-773-3215	500 E. Capitol Pierre, SD 57501-5070	http://www.state.sd.us/attorney/attorney.html

STATE	TELEPHONE	ADDRESS	WEBSITE
Tennessee	615-741-5860	500 Charlotte Ave. Nashville, TN 37243	http://www.attorneygeneral.state.tn.us
Texas	512-463-2100	Capitol Station P.O. Box 12548 Austin, TX 78711-2548	http://www.oag.state.tx.us
Utah,	801-538-9600	State Capitol, Rm. 236, Salt Lake City, UT 84114-0810	http://attorneygeneral.utah.gov/
Vermont	802-828-3173	109 State St. Montpelier, VT 05609-1001	http://www.state.vt.us/atg
Virginia	804-786-2071	900 E. Main St. Richmond, VA 23219	http://www.oag.state.va.us
Washington	360-753-6200	P.O. Box 40100 1125 Washington St. SE, Olympia, WA 98504-0100	http://www.wa.gov/ago
West Virginia	304-558-2021	State Capitol 1900 Kanawha Blvd. E. Charleston, WV 25305	http://www.state.wv.us/wvag
Wisconsin	608-266-1221	State Capitol, Ste. 114 E. P.O. Box 7857 Madison, WI 53707-7857	http://www.doj.state.wi.us
Wyoming	307-777-7841	State Capitol Bldg. Cheyenne, WY 82002	http://attorneygeneral.state.wy.us

APPENDIX 4:
DIRECTORY OF STATE CONSUMER PROTECTION AGENCIES

STATE	ADDRESS	TELEPHONE	FACSIMILE	WEBSITE
Alabama	Consumer Protection Division, Office of the Attorney General, 11 S. Union Street, Montgomery, AL 36130	334-242-7335	n/a	www.ago.state.al.us
Alaska	Consumer Protection Section, Office of the Attorney General, 1031 W. 4th Avenue, Suite 200, Anchorage, AK 99501	907-269-5100	907-276-8554	www.law.state.ak.us
Arizona	Consumer Protection and Advocacy Section, Office of the Attorney General, 1275 W. Washington St., Phoenix, AZ 85007	602-542-3702	602-542-4579	www.ag.state.az.us

STATE	ADDRESS	TELEPHONE	FACSIMILE	WEBSITE
Arkansas	Consumer Protection Division, Office of the Attorney General, 323 Center Street, Suite 200, Little Rock, AR 72201	501-682-2007	501-682-8118	www.ag.state.ar.us
California	Department of Consumer Affairs 400 R Street., Suite 3000, Sacramento, CA 95814	916-445-4465	n/a	www.dist. ct. app.ca.gov
Colorado	Consumer Protection Division, Office of the Attorney General, 1525 Sherman Street, 5th Floor, Denver, CO 80203-1760	303-866-5167	303-866-5443	www.denverda.org
Connecticut	Department of Consumer Protection, 165 Capitol Avenue, Hartford, CT 06106	860-713-6300	860-713-7239	www.state.ct.us/dcp
Delaware	Fraud and Consumer Protection Division, 820 N. French Street, 5th Floor, Wilmington, DE 19801	302-577-8600	302-577-6499	www.state.de.us/ attgen/
District of Columbia	Office of the Corporation Counsel, 441 4the St. N.W., Suite 450-N, Washington, DC 20001	202-442-9828	202-727-6546	n/a

STATE	ADDRESS	TELEPHONE	FACSIMILE	WEBSITE
Florida	Economic Crimes Division, Assistant Deputy Attorney General, PL-01 The Capitol, Tallahassee, FL 32399	850-414-3600	850-414-4483	http://myfloridalegal. com
Georgia	Governor's Office of Consumer Affairs, 2 Martin Luther King Jr. Drive SE, Suite 356, Atlanta, GA 30334	404-656-3790	404-651-9018	www2.state.ga.us/ gaoca
Hawaii	Office of Consumer Protection, 235 South Beretania St., Room 801, Honolulu, HI 96812-3767	808-586-2636	808-586-2640	www.state.hi.us/dcca/
Idaho	Consumer Protection Unit, Attorney General's Office, 650 West State St., Boise, ID 83720-0010	208-334-2424	208-334-2830	www.state.id.us/ag
Illinois	Consumer Protection Division, Office of the Attorney General, 100 W. Randolph Street, 12th Floor, Chicago, IL 60601	312-814-3580	312-814-2549	www.ag.state.il.us
Indiana	Consumer Protection Division, Office of the Attorney General, 402 West Washington Street, 5th Fl., Indianapolis, IN 46204	317-232-6201	317-232-7979	www.in.gov/attorney general

STATE	ADDRESS	TELEPHONE	FACSIMILE	WEBSITE
Iowa	Consumer Protection Division, Office of the Attorney General, 1300 E. Walnut Street, 2nd Floor, Des Moines, IA 50319	515-281-5926	515-281-6771	www.IowaAttorney General.org
Kansas	Consumer Protection Division, Office of the Attorney General, 120 S.W. 10th Street, 4th Floor, Topeka, KS 66612-1597	785-296-3751	785-291-3699	www.ink.org/public/ ksag
Kentucky	Consumer Protection Division, Office of the Attorney General, 1024 Capital Center Dr., Frankfort, KY 40601	502-696-5389	502-573-8317	www.kyattorney general.com/cp
Louisiana	Consumer Protection Section, Office of the Attorney General, 301 Main Street, Suite 1250, Baton Rouge, LA 70801	800-351-4889	225-342-9637	www.ag.state.la.us
Maine	Consumer Mediation Service, Office of the Attorney General, 6 State House Station, Augusta, ME 04333	207-626-8849	207-582-7699	www.state.me.us/ag
Maryland	Consumer Protection Division, Office of the Attorney General, 200 St. Paul Place, 16th Fl., Baltimore, MD 21202-2021	410-528-8662	410-576-7040	www.oag.state.md.us/ consumer

STATE	ADDRESS	TELEPHONE	FACSIMILE	WEBSITE
Massachusetts	Consumer Protection Division, Office of the Attorney General, 200 Portland Street, Boston, MA 02114	617-727-8400	617-727-3265	www.ago.state.ma.us
Michigan	Consumer Protection Division, Office of the Attorney General, P.O. Box 30213, Lansing, MI 48909	517-373-1140	517-241-3771	n/a
Minnesota	Consumer Services Division, Office of the Attorney General, 445 Minnesota Street, St. Paul, MN 55101	612-296-3353	612-282-5801	www.ag.state.mn.us/consumer
Mississippi	Consumer Protection Division, P.O. Box 22947, Jackson, MS 39225-2947	601-359-4230	601-359-4231	www.ago.state.ms.us
Missouri	Consumer Protection and Trade Offense Division, Office of the Attorney General, P.O. Box 899 Jefferson City, MO 65102	573-751-6887	573-751-7948	www.ago.state.mo.us
Montana	Consumer Affairs Unit, 1424 9th Avenue, Helena, MT 59620-0501	406-444-4312	406-444-2903	n/a

STATE	ADDRESS	TELEPHONE	FACSIMILE	WEBSITE
Nebraska	Consumer Protection Division, Department of Justice, 2115 State Capitol, P.O. Box 98920, Lincoln, NE 68509	402-471-2682	402-471-0006	www.nol.org/home/ago
Nevada	Consumer Affairs Division, 1850 East Sahara, Suite 101, Las Vegas, NV 89104	702-486-7355	702-486-7371	www.fyiconsumer.org
New Hampshire	Consumer Protection and Antitrust Division, Office of the Attorney General, 33 Capitol Street, Concord, NH 03301	603-271-3641	603-271-2110	www.state.nh.us/nhd oj/consumer/cpb/html
New Jersey	Division of Consumer Affairs, P.O. Box 45025, Newark, NJ 07101	973-504-6200	n/a	www.state.nj.us/LPs/c a/home.htm
New Mexico	Consumer Protection Division, Office of the Attorney General, P.O. Box Drawer 1508, Santa Fe, NM 87504-1508	505-872-6060	505-827-6685	www.ago.state.nm.us
New York	Bureau of Consumer Frauds and Protection, Office of the Attorney General, State Capitol, Albany, NY 12224	518-474-5481	518-474-3618	www.oag.state.ny.us

STATE	ADDRESS	TELEPHONE	FACSIMILE	WEBSITE
North Carolina	Consumer Protection Division, Office of the Attorney General, P.O. Box 629, Raleigh, NC 27602	919-716-6000	919-716-6050	www.jus.state.nc.us/ cpframe.htm
North Dakota	Consumer Protection and Antitrust Division, Office of the Attorney General, 600 East Boulevard Ave., Department 125, Bismarck, ND 58505-0040	701-328-3404	701-328-2226	www.ag.state.nd.us
Ohio	Consumer Protection Section, Office of the Attorney General, 30 E. Broad Street, 25th Floor, Columbus, OH 43215-3428	614-466-8831	614-728-7583	www.ag.state.oh.us
Oklahoma	Consumer Protection Unit, Office of the Attorney General, 445 N. Lincoln Ave., Oklahoma City, OK 73105	405-521-2029	405-528-1867	www.oag.state.ok.us
Oregon	Consumer Protection Section, Office of the Attorney General, 1162 Court St. N.E., Salem, OR 97310	503-378-4732	503-378-5017	www.doj.state.or.us
Pennsylvania	Bureau of Consumer Protection, Office of the Attorney General, Strawberry Square, 14th Floor, Harrisburg, PA 17120	717-787-9707	717-787-1190	www.attorneygeneral. gov

STATE	ADDRESS	TELEPHONE	FACSIMILE	WEBSITE
Rhode Island	Consumer Protection Unit, Department of the Attorney General, 150 South Main Street, Providence, RI 02903	401-274-4400	401-225-5110	n/a
South Carolina	Department of Consumer Affairs, P.O. Box 11549, Columbia, SC 29211	803-734-3970	803-734-4323	www.scattorneygeneal. org
South Dakota	Division of Consumer Affairs, Office of the Attorney General, 500 East Capitol, Pierre, SD 57501-5070	605-773-4400	605-773-7163	n/a
Tennessee	Division of Consumer Affairs, Department of Commerce & Insurance, 500 James Robertson Parkway, 5th Floor, Nashville, TN 37243-0600	615-741-4737	615-532-4994	www.state.tn.us/ consumer
Texas	Consumer Protection Division, Office of the Attorney General, Box 12548, Capitol Station, Austin, TX 78711	512-463-2185	512-463-8301	www.oag.state.tx.us
Utah	Division of Consumer Protection, Department of Commerce, 160 E. 300th Street, P.O. Box 146704, Salt Lake City, UT 84114-6704	801-530-6601	801-530-6001	www.commerce.state. ut.us

STATE	ADDRESS	TELEPHONE	FACSIMILE	WEBSITE
Vermont	Public Protection Division, Office of the Attorney General, 109 State Street, Montpelier, VT 05609-1001	802-828-5507	n/a	www.state.vt.us/atg
Virginia	Consumer Litigation Section, Office of the Attorney General, 900 East Main Street, Richmond, VA 23219	804-786-2116	804-786-0122	www.oag.state.va.us
Washington	Consumer Resource Center, 900 Fourth Avenue, Suite 2000, Seattle, WA 98164-1012	206-464-6684	206-464-6451	www.wa.gov/ago
West Virginia	Consumer Protection Division, Office of the Attorney General, 812 Quarrier Street 6th Floor, Charleston, WV 25326	304-558-8986	304-558-0184	www.state.wv.us/wvag
Wisconsin	Division of Trade and Consumer Protection, 2811 Agriculture Drive, P.O. Box 8911, Madison, WI 53708	608-224-4953	608-224-4939	www.datcp.state.wi.us
Wyoming	Consumer Protection Unit Office of the Attorney General, 123 State Capitol Building, Cheyenne, WY 82002	307-777-7874	307-777-7956	agwebmaster@state.wy.usattorneygeneral.state.wy.us

APPENDIX 5:
STATE LEMON LAW CONTACTS

STATE	CONTACT	ADDRESS	TELEPHONE
Alabama	Consumer Affairs Section	11 South Union St., Montgomery, AL 36130-0152	(334) 242-7334
Alaska	Fair Business Section	1031 West 4th Ave. Ste. 200, Anchorage, AK 99508	(907) 269-5100
Arizona	None Listed		
Arkansas	Consumer Protection Division	200 Tower Building, 323 Center St., Little Rock, Arkansas 72201-2610	(501) 682-2341
California	The Arbitration Certification Program	400 R St. Suite 201 Sacramento, CA 95814	(916) 323-3406
Colorado	Colorado Dealer Licensing Board	none listed	(303) 205-5605
Connecticut	Department of Consumer Protection	165 Capitol Avenue, Hartford, CT 06106	(860) 713-6120
Delaware	Office of the Attorney General	820 N. French St., Wilmington, DE 19801	(302) 577-8600
District of Columbia	Department of Consumer and Regulatory Affairs	941 North Capitol St. NE Washington, DC 20002	(202) 442-4400
Florida	Division of Consumer Services	2005 Apalachee Parkway Tallahassee, Fl 32399-6500	(850) 922-2966

STATE	CONTACT	ADDRESS	TELEPHONE
Georgia	The Governor's Office of Consumer Affairs	2 M.L. King Jr. Dr., Suite 356, Atlanta, GA 30334	(404) 656-3790
Hawaii	Department of Commerce and Consumer Affairs, State Certified Arbitration Program	235 S. Beretania St., 9th Floor, Honolulu, HI 96813	(808) 587-3222
Idaho	Office of the Attorney General	700 W. Jefferson St., P.O. Box 83720, Boise, Idaho 83720-0010	(208) 334-2424
Illinois	Office of the Attorney General	500 South Second St., Springfield, Illinois 62706	(217) 782-1090
Indiana	Office of Indiana Attorney General	402 West Washington St., IGCS-Fifth Floor Indianapolis, Indiana 46204	(317) 232-6201
Iowa	Consumer Protection Division	1305 East Walnut St., Des Moines, Iowa 50319	(515) 281-5926
Kansas	Consumer Protection Division	Kansas Judicial Center, Topeka, Kansas 66612	(800) 432-2310
Kentucky	Consumer Protection Division	1024 Capital Center Drive Frankfort, Kentucky 40601	(502) 696-5389
Louisiana	Consumer Protection Division	State Capitol, 22nd Floor, Baton Rouge, Louisiana 70804-9005	(225) 342-7013
Maine	Lemon Law Arbitration Program	6 State House Station, Augusta, Maine 04333-0006	(207) 626-8848

STATE	CONTACT	ADDRESS	TELEPHONE
Maryland	Consumer Protection Division	200 Saint Paul Place, 16th Floor Baltimore, MD 21202	(410) 528-8662
Massachusetts	Office of Consumer Affairs and Business Regulation	1 Ashburton Place, Room 1411, Boston, MA 02108	(617) 727-7780
Michigan	Consumer Protection Division,	P.O. Box 30213, Lansing, MI 48909	(517) 373-1140
Minnesota	Consumer Protection Division	445 Minnesota St., St. Paul, MN 55101	(612) 296-3353
Mississippi	Office of the Attorney General	P.O. Box 22947, Jackson, Mississippi 39225-2947	(601) 359-4230 1-800-281-4418 in Mississippi
Missouri	Attorney General's Office	Supreme Court Building, 207 W. High St., Jefferson City, MO 65102	(573) 751-3321
Montana	Consumer Affairs Section	P.O. Box 200501, Helena, MT 59620	(406) 444-3553
Nebraska	Department of Motor Vehicles, Legal Division	P.O. Box 94789, Lincoln NE 68509-4789	(402) 471-9593
Nevada	Attorney General	100 North Carson St., Carson City, Nevada 89701-4717	(775) 684-1100
New Hampshire	New Motor Vehicle Arbitration Board	10 Hazen Drive, Concord, NH 03305	(603) 271-6383
New Jersey	Division of Consumer Affairs, Lemon Law Unit	P.O. Box 45026, Newark, New Jersey 07101	(973) 504-6226
New Mexico	Consumer Protection Division	P.O. Drawer 1508, Santa Fe, NM 87504-1508	(505) 827-6060
New York	Consumer Protection Division	120 Broadway, New York, NY 10271	(212) 416-8000

STATE	CONTACT	ADDRESS	TELEPHONE
North Carolina	Consumer Protection Section	P.O. Box 629, Raleigh, NC 27602-0629	(919) 716-600
North Dakota	Consumer Protection Division	600 E. Boulevard Ave., Dept 125, Bismarck, ND 58505-0040	(701) 328-3404
Ohio	Consumer Protection Section	30 E. Broad St., 25th Floor, Columbus, Ohio 43215-3428	none listed
Oklahoma	Consumer Protection Unit	4545 N. Lincoln Blvd., #260, Oklahoma City, OK 73105	(405) 521-3921
Oregon	Financial Fraud/ Consumer Protection Section	1162 Court St. N.E., Salem, OR 97310	(503) 378-4320
Pennsylvania.	Office of Attorney General	Strawberry Square, 16th Floor, Harrisburg, PA 17120	(717) 787-3391
Rhode Island	Office of the Attorney General	150 South Main St., Providence, RI 02903	(401) 274-4400
South Carolina	Office of the Attorney General	P.O. Box 11549, Columbia, SC 29211	(803) 734-3970
South Dakota	Division of Consumer Protection	500 East Capitol, Pierre, SD 57501	(605) 773-4400
Tennessee	Division of Consumer Affairs	500 James Robertson Parkway, Fifth Floor, Nashville, TN 37243-0600	(615) 741-4737
Texas	Consumer Affairs Section	P.O. Box 2293, Austin, Texas 78768-2293	(512) 416-4800
Utah	Division of Consumer Protection	160 East 300 South, Box 146704, Salt Lake City, Utah 84114-6704	(801) 530-6601

STATE	CONTACT	ADDRESS	TELEPHONE
Vermont	Motor Vehicle Arbitration Board	120 State St., Montpelier, VT 05603-0001	(802) 828-2943
Virginia	Office of the Attorney General	900 East Main St., Richmond, VA 23219	(804) 786-2071
Washington	Lemon Law Administration	900 4th Ave. Ste. 2000 Seattle, WA 98164-1012	(800) 541-8898
West Virginia	Consumer Protection Division	1900 Kanawha Blvd. Room 26E Charleton, WV 25305-9924	(304) 558-2021
Wisconsin	Wisconsin Department of Transportation, Dealer Section	P.O. Box 7909 Madison, WI 53707-7909	(608) 266-1425
Wyoming	Office of the Attorney General	123 Capitol Building Cheyenne, WY 82002	(307) 777-7841

APPENDIX 6:
VEHICLES COVERED UNDER
STATE LEMON LAWS

STATE	VEHICLES COVERED
Alabama	Every vehicle intended primarily for use and operation on the public highways that is self-propelled. Excludes motor homes or any vehicle with a GVW of 10,000 pounds or more.
Alaska	Any land vehicle having four or more wheels, that is self-propelled by a motor, is normally used for personal, family, or household purposes, and is required to be registered. Does not include a tractor, farm vehicle, or a vehicle designed primarily for off-road use.
Arizona	A self-propelled vehicle designated primarily for the transportation of persons or property over the public highways. Only the chassis portion of a motor home is covered.
Arkansas	Any self-propelled vehicle licensed, purchased, or leased and primarily designed for the transportation of persons or property over the public streets and highways, but does not include mopeds, motorcycles, the living facilities of a motor home, or vehicles over 10,000 pounds GVW. The 10,000 pound limit does not apply to motor homes.
California	A new motor vehicle that is used or bought for use primarily for personal, family, or household purposes. Includes the chassis portion of motor homes.
Colorado	A self-propelled private passenger vehicle, including pickup trucks and vans, designed primarily for travel on the public highways and used to carry not more than 10 persons. Excludes motor homes and motorcycles.
Connecticut	Passenger and commercial motor vehicles.
Delaware	Passenger motor vehicles. Does not include motor homes (other than the chassis) or motorcycles.
District of Columbia	Any vehicle sold or registered that is designed for transporting persons. Excludes buses, motorcycles, motor homes and recreational vehicles.

STATE	VEHICLES COVERED
Florida	A new vehicle that is purchased or leased primarily for personal, family, or household purposes. Does not include vehicles run only on tracks, off-road vehicles, trucks over ten thousand pounds gross weight, the living facilities of recreational vehicles or motorcycles or mopeds.
Georgia	Any self-propelled vehicle, primarily designed for the transportation of persons or property over the public highways, that was leased, purchased or registered. Applies only to the chassis portion of motor homes. Does not include motorcycles or trucks with 10,000 pounds or more GVW.
Hawaii	A self-propelled vehicle primarily designed for the transportation of persons or property over public streets and highways which is used primarily for personalfamily, or household purposes. Does not include mopeds, motorcycles, or motor scooters, or vehicles over 10,000 pounds GVW.
Idaho	A new motor vehicle used for personal business use or personal, family or household purposes. Does not include a motorcycle, farm tractor, trailer or any motor vehicle with a gross laden weight over 12,000 pounds.
Illinois	New cars. Light trucks and vans under 8,000 pounds. Recreational vehicles excluding trailers. Excludes motorcycles.
Indiana	Any self-propelled vehicle that has a declared gross vehicle weight of less than 10,000 pounds and is intended primarily for use and operation on public highways. Does not include conversion vans, motor homes, farm machinery, motorcycles, mopeds, snowmobiles, or vehicles designed primarily for off-road use.
Iowa	A self-propelled vehicle purchased or leased and primarily designed for the transportation of persons or property over public streets and highways, but does not include mopeds, motorcycles, motor homes, or vehicles over ten thousand pounds GVW.
Kansas	A new motor vehicle which is sold or leased, and which is registered for a gross weight of 12,000 pounds or less. Does not include the customized parts of motor vehicles that have been added or modified by second stage manufacturers, first stage converters or second stage converters.
Kentucky	All vehicles except conversion vans, motor homes, mopeds, motorcycles, farm machinery and vehicles with more than 2 axles.
Louisiana	All vehicles under 10,000 pounds except motor homes, motorcycles, and vehicles used for commercial purposes only.
Maine	Any vehicle purchased or leased. Excludes commercial vehicles over 8,000 pounds.

STATE	VEHICLES COVERED
Maryland	Any passenger car or truck with a rated capacity of 1 ton or less.
Massachusetts	All vehicles, except off-road vehicles, motor homes, motorcycles, and vehicles used for commercial purposes.
Michigan	Any new car, van or truck bought by a resident of Michigan for personal or family use.
Minnesota	A new motor vehicle used for personal, family, or household purposes at least 40 percent of the time.
Mississippi	Vehicles used primarily for personal, family or household purposes. Excludes off-road vehicles, mopeds, and motorcycles. Includes motor home chassis.
Missouri	A new motor vehicle, primarily used for personal, family, or household purposes. Does not include commercial vehicles, off-road vehicles, mopeds, motorcycles or recreational vehicles.
Montana	Any vehicle, including the nonresidential portion of a motor home, propelled by its own power, designed primarily to transport persons or property upon the public highways. Does not include trucks with 10,000 pounds or more GVW or motorcycles.
Nebraska	A new motor vehicle normally used for personal, family, household, or business purposes, excluding motor homes.
Nevada	A new motor vehicle normally used for personal, family or household purposes, except a motor home or off-road vehicle.
New Hampshire	Any 4-wheel motor vehicle with a gross weight not exceeding 9,000 pounds. Also includes off highway recreational vehicles, mopeds and motorcycles.
New Jersey	Passenger automobiles and motorcycles. Includes the non-living portions of motor homes.
New Mexico	A passenger motor vehicle including an automobile, pickup truck, motorcycle or van normally used for personal, family or household purposes with a gross vehicle weight less than 10,000 pounds.
New York	Any non-commercial motor vehicle purchased or leased, except for motorcycles, certain motor homes, and off-road vehicles.
North Carolina	Any new motor vehicle other than a house trailer, provided that the vehicle does not have a gross vehicle weight of 10,000 pounds or more. This includes pickup trucks, motorcycles and most vans.
North Dakota	Passenger motor vehicles and trucks 10,000 pounds GVW or less, normally used for personal, family or household purposes.

STATE	VEHICLES COVERED
Ohio	Passenger car, light truck (no more than one ton load capacity and not used in business), or motorcycle. Also includes chassis portion of motor homes.
Oklahoma	Any motor driven vehicle required to be registered, excluding vehicles above 10,000 pounds GVW and the living facilities of motor homes.
Oregon	A new motor vehicle normally used for personal, family or household purposes.
Pennsylvania	Vehicles used primarily for personal, family or household purposes except motor homes, motorcycles, and off-road vehicles.
Rhode Island	An automobile, truck, motorcycle, or van having a gross vehicle weight of less than 10,000 pounds.
South Carolina	Passenger motor vehicles including cars, vans, and small trucks.
South Dakota	All vehicles intended primarily for use and operation on the public highways that is self-propelled. Does not include motor homes or vehicles with a GVW of 10,000 pounds or more.
Tennessee	Any motor vehicle not including motorized bicycles, motor homes, recreational vehicles or off-road vehicles and vehicles over 10,000 pounds GVW.
Texas	New vehicles, including cars, trucks, vans, motorcycles, all-terrain vehicles, motor homes and towable recreational vehicles.
Utah	A car or truck weighing less than 12,000 pounds or a motor home.
Vermont	Passenger motor vehicles and trucks under 10,000 pounds GVW. Does not include snowmobiles, motorcycles, mopeds, or the living portion of recreational vehicles.
Virginia	A motor vehicle used in substantial part for personal, family, or household purposes.
Washington	Any new self-propelled vehicle, including a new motorcycle, primarily designed for the transportation of persons or property over the public highways. Does not include living portions of motor homes or trucks with 19,000 or more GVW.
West Virginia	Passenger vehicles, pickup trucks, vans and motor home chassis used primarily for personal, family, or household purposes.
Wisconsin	All vehicles except mopeds, semi-trailers or trailers designed for use in combination with a truck or truck tractor.
Wyoming	All vehicles under 10,000 lbs. GVW.

APPENDIX 7:
COVERAGE PERIOD UNDER
STATE LEMON LAWS

STATE	COVERAGE PERIOD
Alabama	1 year or 12,000 miles
Alaska	Warranty period or 1 year
Arizona	Warranty period, 2 years or 24,000 miles
Arkansas	2 years or 24,000 miles
California	18 months or 18,000 miles
Colorado	Warranty period or 1 year
Connecticut	2 years or 18,000 miles
Delaware	Warranty period or 1 year
District of Columbia	2 years or 18,000 miles
Florida	18 months or 24,000 miles
Georgia	1 year or 12,000 miles
Hawaii	Warranty period, 2 years or 24,000 miles
Idaho	Warranty period, 2 years or 24,000 miles
Illinois	1 year or 12,000 miles
Indiana	18 months or 18,000 miles
Iowa	2 years or 24,000 miles
Kansas	Warranty period or 1 year
Kentucky	1 year or 12,000 miles
Louisiana	Warranty period or 1 year
Maine	2 years or 18,000 miles
Maryland	15 months or 15,000 miles 12 months or 12,000 miles for leased vehicles
Massachusetts	1 year or 15,000 miles

STATE	COVERAGE PERIOD
Michigan	Warranty period or 1 year
Minnesota	Warranty period or 2 years
Mississippi	Warranty period or 1 year
Missouri	Warranty period or 1 year
Montana	2 years or 18,000 miles
Nebraska	Warranty period or 1 year
Nevada	Warranty period or 1 year
New Hampshire	Warranty period plus 1 year
New Jersey	2 years or 18,000 miles
New Mexico	Warranty period or 1 year
New York	2 years or 18,000 miles
North Carolina	2 years or 24,000 miles
North Dakota	Warranty period or 1 year
Ohio	1 year or 18,000 miles
Oklahoma	Warranty period or 1 year
Oregon	1 year or 12,000 miles
Pennsylvania	Warranty period, 1 year or 12,000 miles
Rhode Island	1 year or 15,000 miles
South Carolina	1 year or 12,000 miles
South Dakota	1 year or 12,000 miles
Tennessee	Warranty period or 1 year
Texas	Warranty period or 1 year
Utah	Warranty period or 1 year
Vermont	Warranty period
Virginia	18 months
Washington	2 years or 24,000 miles
West Virginia	Warranty period or 1 year
Wisconsin	Warranty period or 1 year
Wyoming	1 year

APPENDIX 8:
DIRECTORY OF STATE LEMON LAW
REPAIR ATTEMPTS AND INTERVALS

STATE	REPAIR INTERVAL
Alabama	3 repair attempts or 30 calendar days out of service
Alaska	3 repair attempts or 30 business days out of service
Arizona	4 repair attempts or 30 calendar days out of service
Arkansas	1 repair attempt for a defect that might cause death or serious injury; 3 repair attempts for the same defect; or 5 repair attempts for separate problems; or 30 calendar days out of service
California	2 repair attempts for a defect that might cause death or serious injury or 4 repair attempts or 30 calendar days out of service
Colorado	4 repair attempts or 30 business days out of service
Connecticut	4 repair attempts or 30 calendar days out of service
Delaware	4 repair attempts or 30 business days out of service
District of Columbia	4 repair attempts or 30 days out of service
Florida	3 repair attempts or 30 calendar days out of service
Georgia	1 repair attempt in the braking or steering system; 3 repair attempts; or 30 calendar days out of service for other problems
Hawaii	1 repair attempt for a defect that might cause death or serious injury; 3 repair attempts; or 30 business days out of service
Idaho	4 repair attempts or 30 business days out of service
Illinois	4 repair attempts or 30 business days out of service
Indiana	4 repair attempts or 30 business days out of service
Iowa	1 repair attempt for a defect that might cause death or serious injury; 3 repair attempts; or 30 calendar days out of service for other problems

STATE	REPAIR INTERVAL
Kansas	4 repair attempts for the same defect; 10 repair attempts for separate problems; or 30 calendar days out of service
Kentucky	4 repair attempts or 30 days out of service
Louisiana	4 repair attempts or 30 calendar days out of service
Maine	3 repair attempts or 15 business days out of service
Maryland	1 repair attempt in the braking or steering system; 4 repair attempts; or 30 calendar days out of service for other problems
Massachusetts	3 repair attempts or 15 business days out of service
Michigan	4 repair attempts or 30 business days out of service
Minnesota	1 repair attempt in the braking or steering system; 4 repair attempts; or 30 business days out of service for other problems
Mississippi	3 repair attempts or 15 business days out of service
Missouri	4 repair attempts or 30 business days out of service
Montana	4 repair attempts or 30 business days out of service
Nebraska	4 repair attempts or 40 days out of service
Nevada	4 repair attempts or 30 calendar days out of service
New Hampshire	3 repair attempts or 30 business days out of service
New Jersey	3 repair attempts or 30 calendar days out of service
New Mexico	4 repair attempts or 30 business days out of service
New York	4 repair attempts or 30 calendar days out of service
North Carolina	4 repair attempts or more than 20 days out of service during any 12 month period
North Dakota	3 repair attempts or 30 business days out of service
Ohio	3 repair attempts; 30 calendar days out of service; 8 repair attempts for different problems; or 1 attempt to repair condition likely to cause death or serious bodily injury
Oklahoma	4 repair attempts or 45 days out of service
Oregon	4 repair attempts or 30 business days out of service
Pennsylvania	3 repair attempts or 30 calendar days out of service
Rhode Island	4 repair attempts or 30 calendar days out of service
South Carolina	3 repair attempts or 30 calendar days out of service
South Dakota	4 repair attempts plus 1 final attempt
Tennessee	4 repair attempts or 30 calendar days out of service

STATE	REPAIR INTERVAL
Texas	4 repair attempts; 30 days out of service; or 2 repair attempts for a serious safety hazard
Utah	4 repair attempts or 30 business days out of service
Vermont	3 repair attempts or 30 calendar days out of service
Virginia	3 repair attempts; 30 calendar days out of service; or 1 repair attempt for a serious safety defect
Washington	4 repair attempts; 30 calendar days out of service; or 2 attempts for a serious safety defect
West Virginia	3 repair attempts; 30 calendar days out of service; or 1 attempt for a condition likely to cause death or serious bodily injury
Wisconsin	4 repair attempts or 30 days out of service
Wyoming	3 repair attempts or 30 business days out of service

APPENDIX 9:
DIRECTORY OF NATIONAL CONSUMER ORGANIZATIONS

ORGANIZATION	ADDRESS	TELEPHONE	FACSIMILE	EMAIL	WEBSITE	FUNCTION
AARP Consumer Protection	601 E. St. NW, Washington, DC 20049	202-434-3410	202-434-6470	n/a	www.aarp.org	The Consumer Protection unit is charged by the AARP to examine those consumer problems and issues that impact the financial security of people 50 years of age and older, and to help its members protect themselves from marketplace fraud and deception. To this end, Consumer Protection stays abreast of current and breaking consumer developments, and employs a variety of strategies to inform AARP members.

ORGANIZATION	ADDRESS	TELEPHONE	FACSIMILE	EMAIL	WEBSITE	FUNCTION
Alliance Against Fraud in Telemarketing and Electronic Commerce (AAFTEC) National Consumers League	1701 K St. NW, Suite 1200, Washington, DC 20006	202-835-3323	202-835-0747	info@nclnet. org	www.nclnet. org	The Alliance, coordinated by the National Consumers League, is a coalition of public interest groups, trade associations, labor unions, businesses, law enforcement agencies, educators, and consumer protection agencies. AAFTEC members promote efforts to educate the public about telemarketing and Internet fraud, and how consumers can shop safely by phone and online.
American Council on Consumer Interests (ACCI)	415 South Duff, Ste. C, Ames, IA 50010-6600	515-956-4666	515-233-3101	info@consume rinterests.org	www.consum erinterests. org	Serving the professional needs of consumer educators, researchers, and policymakers, ACCI publications and educational programs foster the production, synthesis, and dissemination of information in the consumer interest.
American Council on Science and Health (ACSH)	1995 Broadway, 2nd Floor, New York, NY 10023-5860	212-362-7044	212-362-4919	acsh@acsh. org	www.acsh.org	A nonprofit public education group, ACSH has the goal to provide consumers with up-to-date scientifically sound information on the relationship between human health and chemicals, foods, lifestyles, and the environment. Booklets and special reports on a variety of topics are available, as is a quarterly magazine: Priorities.

ORGANIZATION	ADDRESS	TELEPHONE	FACSIMILE	EMAIL	WEBSITE	FUNCTION
Center for Science in the Public Interest (CSPI)	1875 Connecticut Ave. NW, Suite 300, Washington, DC 20009	202-332-9110	202-265-4954	cspi@cspinet. org	www.cspinet. org	A nonprofit, membership organization, CSPI conducts research, education, and advocacy on nutrition, health, food safety and related issues, and publishes the monthly Nutrition Action Healthletter as well as other consumer information materials.
Center for the Study of Services	733 15th St. NW, Washington, DC 20005	202-347-7283	202-347-4000	n/a	www.check book.org	Nonprofit organization publishes books and pamphlets to help consumers select doctors, hospitals, and health plans. Publishes pamphlets and offers services to help consumers get good prices on new cars. Publishes information and maintains on-line database to help consumers shop for good prices and desired features in big-ticket products — audio-video, major appliances, sporting goods, tires, home-office, etc.

ORGANIZATION	ADDRESS	TELEPHONE	FACSIMILE	EMAIL	WEBSITE	FUNCTION
Coalition Against Insurance Fraud	1012 14th St. NW, Suite 200, Washington, DC 20005	202-393-7330	202-393-7329	info@insur-ancefraud.org	www.Insur-anceFraud.org	The Coalition Against Insurance Fraud is a national alliance of consumer groups, government agencies, and insurance companies dedicated to combating all forms of insurance fraud through advocacy and public information. It conducts research, develops public education programs and publishes a consumer brochure, How to Avoid Becoming a Victim of Insurance Fraud, which is available upon request. It also refers consumers to appropriate agencies to report incidences of insurance fraud.
Community Nutrition Institute (CNI)	41156 45th Ave., Wahkon, MN 56386	320-676-8753	320-676-3066	n/a	n/a	An advocate for programs and services to enable consumers to enjoy a diet that is adequate, safe, and healthy. CNI also works to increase citizen participation in the state and Federal policy and administrative processes to achieve these goals. CNI publishes Nutrition Week, a newsletter covering nutrition and food safety issues, as well as related legislative and regulatory actions.

ORGANIZATION	ADDRESS	TELEPHONE	FACSIMILE	EMAIL	WEBSITE	FUNCTION
Congress Watch	215 Pennsylvania Ave. SE, Washington, DC 20003	202-546-4996	202-547-7392	congresswatch @citizen.org	www.citizen. org	An arm of Public Citizen, Congress Watch works for consumer-related legislation, regulation, and policies in such areas as health and safety, and campaign financing, and has publications available on the issues with which it deals.
Consumer Action	717 Market St., Suite 310, San Francisco, CA 94103	415-777-9635	415-777-5267	info@consume r-action.org	www.consum er-action.org	Consumer Action assists consumers with marketplace problems. An education and advocacy organization specializing in credit, finance, and telecommunications issues. Consumer Action offers a multi-lingual consumer complaint hotline, free information on its surveys of banks and long-distance telephone companies, and consumer education materials in as many as eight languages. Community based organizations can receive these free publications in bulk.

ORGANIZATION	ADDRESS	TELEPHONE	FACSIMILE	EMAIL	WEBSITE	FUNCTION
Consumer Alert	1001 Connecticut Ave. NW, Suite 1128, Washington, DC 20036	202-467-5809	202-467-5814	info@consumeralert.org	www.consumeralert.org	Consumer Alert's mission is to inform the public about the consumer benefits of competitive enterprise and to expose the flawed economic, scientific and risk data that underlie certain public policies. Consumer Alert has an active program of consumers with information to help them make every day decisions. The constituent of Consumer Alert is the real consumer who pays the bills.
Consumer Federation of America (CFA)	1424 16th St. NW, Suite 604, Washington, DC 20036	202-387-6121	202-265-7989	n/a	www.consumerfed.org	Comprised of more than 240 organizations representing a membership exceeding 50 million consumers, CFA is a consumer advocacy and education organization. Issues on which it currently represents consumer interests before Congress and Federal regulatory agencies include telephone service, insurance and financial services, product safety, indoor air pollution, health care, product liability, and utility rates. It develops and distributes studies of various consumer issues, as well as consumer guides in book and pamphlet form. In addition, CFA publishes several newsletters.

ORGANIZATION	ADDRESS	TELEPHONE	FACSIMILE	EMAIL	WEBSITE	FUNCTION
Consumers for World Trade (CWT)	1001 Connecticut Ave. N.W., Suite 1110, Washington, DC 20036	202-293-2944	202-293-0495	cwt@cwt.org	www.cwt.org	A nonprofit organization, CWT supports trade expansion and liberalization to promote economic growth and increase consumer choice and price competition in the marketplace. Various publications are available.
Families USA Foundation	1334 G St. NW, Suite 300, Washington, DC 20005-3169	202-628-3030	202-347-2417	info@families usa.org	www.families usa.org	A national, nonprofit membership organization committed to comprehensive reform of health and long-term care. Families USA works to educate and mobilize consumers on health care issues. In addition to its two grass roots advocacy networks—asap!, a network of health and long-term care reform activists and HealthLink USA, a nationwide health reform computer network for public interest groups —Families USA develops and distributes reports and other materials on health and long-term care issues.

ORGANIZATION	ADDRESS	TELEPHONE	FACSIMILE	EMAIL	WEBSITE	FUNCTION
HALT: An Organization of Americans for Legal Reform	1612 K St. NW, Suite 510, Washington, DC 20006	202-887-8255	202-887-9699	halt@halt.org	www.halt.org	HALT's mission is to enable Americans to handle their legal affairs affordably, equitably, and simply. HALT publishes a series of self-help legal manuals, operates a legal information clearinghouse, and advocates for legal reforms which will benefit consumers.
Health Research Group (HRG)	1600 20th St. NW, Washington, DC 20009	202-588-1000	n/a	n/a	www.citizen.org/hrg	A division of Public Citizen, HRG works for protection against unsafe foods, drugs, medical devices, and workplaces, and advocates for greater consumer control over personal health decisions. A monthly Health Letter and a monthly letter on prescription drugs are available.
Jump$tart Coalition for Personal Financial Literacy	919 18th St. NW, Suite 300, Washington, DC 20006	202-466-8610	202-223-0321	info@jump-startcoalition.org	www.jumpstart.org	The Coalition's direct objective is to encourage curriculum enrichment to ensure that basic personal financial management skills are attained during the K-12 educational experience.

ORGANIZATION	ADDRESS	TELEPHONE	FACSIMILE	EMAIL	WEBSITE	FUNCTION
National Association of Consumer Agency Administrators (NACAA)	1010 Vermont Ave. NW, Suite 514, Washington, DC 20005	202-347-7395	202-347-2563	nacaa@erols. com	www.nacaa-net.org	An association of the administrators of local, state, and Federal Government consumer protection agencies, NACAA provides training programs, public policy studies and conferences, professional publications, and other member services.
The National Association of Proactive Consumers (NAPC)	P.O. Box 1948, Dover, DE 19903	800-726-0727	n/a	n/a	www.napc.net	n/a
National Coalition for Consumer Education	1701 K Street NW, Suite 1200, Washington, DC 20006	202-835-3323	202-835-0747	n/a	www.nclnet.org	NCCE is a coalition coordinated by the National Consumers League. It develops and provides educational materials and resources to consumer educators through a network of state coordinators. The coalition sponsors LifeSmarts, a game-show competition open to all teens in the United States who are in the 9th through 12th grade.

ORGANIZATION	ADDRESS	TELEPHONE	FACSIMILE	EMAIL	WEBSITE	FUNCTION
National Community Reinvestment Coalition (NCRC)	733 15th St. NW, Suite 540, Washington, DC 20005	202-628-8866	202-628-9800	member@ncrc. org	www.ncrc.org	NCRC was founded in 1990 with the goal of ending discriminatory banking practices and increasing the flow of private capital and credit into underserved communities across the country. NCRC has over 600 members in every state and major city in America as well as in many smaller cities and rural areas.
National Consumer Law Center (NCLC)	77 Summer St., 10th Floor, Boston, MA 02111-1006	617-542-8010	617-523-7398	consumerlaw @nclc.org	www.con- sumerlaw.org	NCLC is an advocacy and research organization focusing on the needs of low-income consumers. It represents the interests of consumers in court, before administrative agencies, and before legislatures. The Center also publishes Surviving Debt: A Guide for Consumers and the Consumer Credit and Sales Legal Practice Series consisting of thirteen desk reference manuals for attorneys.

ORGANIZATION	ADDRESS	TELEPHONE	FACSIMILE	EMAIL	WEBSITE	FUNCTION
National Consumers League	1701 K St. NW, Suite 1200, Washington, DC 20006	202-835-3323	202-835-0747	info@nclnet. org	www.nclnet. org	Founded in 1899, the mission of the NCL is to identify, protect, represent, and advance the economic and social interests of consumers and workers. The league is a nonprofit membership organization working for health, safety, and fairness in the marketplace and workplace. Current principal issue areas include consumer fraud, food and drug safety, fair labor standards, child labor, health care, the environment, financial services and telecommunications. The league develops and distributes consumer education materials and newsletters.

ORGANIZATION	ADDRESS	TELEPHONE	FACSIMILE	EMAIL	WEBSITE	FUNCTION
National Fraud Center	1701 K St. NW, Ste. 1200, Washington, DC 20006	800-876-7060	202-835-0767	n/a	www.fraud. org	NFC/IFW assists consumers with recognizing and filing complaints about telemarketing and Internet fraud. A project of the National Consumers League, the hotline provides consumers with information to help them avoid becoming victims of fraud, and assistance in relaying consumers' reports about telemarketing and Internet to the appropriate law enforcement agencies. Spanish-speaking counselors available.
National Institute for Consumer Education (NICE)	G12 Boone Halle, Eastern Michigan University, Ypsilanti, MI 48197	734-487-2292	734-487-7153	gwen.reich-bach@emich. edu	www.nice. emich.edu	NICE is a consumer education resource and professional development center for K-12 classroom teachers, business, government, labor, and community educators. NICE conducts training programs, develops teaching guides and resource lists, and manages a national clearinghouse of consumer education materials, including videos, software programs, textbooks, and curriculum guides.

ORGANIZATION	ADDRESS	TELEPHONE	FACSIMILE	EMAIL	WEBSITE	FUNCTION
Professional Consumer Advocates Inc.	P.O. Box 1948, Dover, DE 19903	302-672-7945	n/a	advantage@pcasafety.net	www.pcasafety.net	A consulting practice assisting consumers with the review of debt collection, telemarketing, and automobile and insurance practices. Professional Consumer Advocates is a membership organization encouraging consumers to be proactive.
Public Citizen, Inc.	1600 20th St. NW, Washington, DC 20009	202-588-1000	202-588-7799	pcmail@citizen.org	www.citizen.org	A national, nonprofit membership organization representing consumer interests through lobbying, litigation, research, and publications. Public Citizen represents consumer interests in Congress, the courts, government agencies, and the media. Primary current areas of interest include product liability, health care delivery, safe medical devices and medications, open and ethical government, and safe and sustainable energy use.

ORGANIZATION	ADDRESS	TELEPHONE	FACSIMILE	EMAIL	WEBSITE	FUNCTION
Self Help for Hard of Hearing People	7910 Woodmont Ave, Suite 1200, Bethesda, MD 20814	301-657-2248	301-913-9413	national@shhh.org	www.shhh.org	The largest international consumer organization devoted to serving the interests of consumers with hearing loss through self help, advocacy, and education. Founded in 1979, SHHH is a non-profit membership association with over 250 chapters throughout the U.S. Publications include information on: hearing aids, cochlear implants, assistive listening devices, Americans with Disabilities Act, employment, travel, lip-reading, education, parenting, medical research, psychological stress and telephone and television strategies. Holds annual conventions and publishes Hearing Loss: The Journal of Self Help for Hard of Hearing People.

ORGANIZATION	ADDRESS	TELEPHONE	FACSIMILE	EMAIL	WEBSITE	FUNCTION
Society of Consumer Affairs Professionals in Business (SOCAP)	675 North Washington St., Suite 200, Alexandria, VA 22314	703-519-3700	703-549-4886	socap@socap. org	www.socap. org	An international professional organization, SOCAP provides training, conferences and publications to encourage and maintain the integrity of business in transactions with consumers; to encourage and promote effective communication and understanding among business, government and consumers; and to define and advance the consumer affairs profession.
U.S. Public Interest Research Group (U.S. PIRG)	218 D St. SE, Washington, DC 20003-1900	202-546-9707	202-546-2461	uspirg@pirg. org	www.pirg.org	U.S. PIRG is the national lobbying office for the state public interest research groups. The PIRGs are consumer environmental advocacy groups active in many states across the country. U.S. PIRG works on a variety of consumer and environmental protection issues, including bank fees, credit bureau abuses, clean air and clean water, right to know, campaign finance reform, and various other issues. U.S. PIRG does not handle individual consumer complaints directly but measures complaint levels to gauge the need for remedial legislation.

ORGANIZATION	ADDRESS	TELEPHONE	FACSIMILE	EMAIL	WEBSITE	FUNCTION
United Seniors Health Cooperative (USHC)	300 D Street, Suite 801 SW, Washington, DC 20024-3212	202-479-1200	202-479-6660	ushc@unitedse niorshealth.org	www.unitedse niorshealth. org	USHC is a nonprofit membership organization that provides consumer tested information to help seniors achieve good health, independence, and financial security. Publications include books on long-term care planning, managing health care finances, and choosing an HMO. Professionals working with low-income persons of all ages will find USHC's benefit screening software valuable for a quick, comprehensive determination of a person's eligibility for public benefits and assistance programs

APPENDIX 10:
NATIONAL DIRECTORY OF BETTER BUSINESS BUREAUS

STATE	ADDRESS	TELEPHONE	FAX	EMAIL	WEBSITE
Alabama	National Headquarters Council of Better Business Bureaus Inc., 4200 Wilson Boulevard, Suite 800, Arlington, VA 22203	703-276-0100	703-525-8277	n/a	www.bbb.org

STATE	ADDRESS	TELEPHONE	FAX	EMAIL	WEBSITE
Alabama	Better Business Bureau, 600 College Street, Albertville, AL 35950	256-878-0041	n/a	info@northalabama.bbb.org	www.northalabama.bbb.org
Alabama	Better Business Bureau, PO Box 55268, Birmingham, AL 35255-5268	205-558-2222	205-558-2239	info@birmingham-al.bbb.org	www.birmingham-al.bbb.org
Alabama	Better Business Bureau, 2528 Spring Ave, SW, Decatur, AL 35601	n/a	n/a	info@northalabama.bbb.org	www.northalabama.bbb.org
Alabama	Better Business Bureau, 118 Woodburn Road, Dothan, AL 36305	334-794-0492	334-794-0659	info@dothan.bbb.org	n/a

STATE	ADDRESS	TELEPHONE	FAX	EMAIL	WEBSITE
Alabama	Better Business Bureau, 205 South Seminary St., Suite 114, Florence, AL 35630	256-533-1640	256-740-8219	bbbshoal@hiwaay. net	www.northalaba-ma.bbb.org
Alabama	Better Business Bureau, 300 Gault Ave. North, Fort Payne, AL 35967,	n/a	n/a	info@northalaba ma.bbb.org	www.northalabam a.bbb.org
Alabama	Better Business Bureau, P.O. Box 383, Huntsville, AL 35804	256-533-1640	n/a	info@northalaba ma.bbb.org	www.northalaba-ma.bbb.org
Alabama	Better Business Bureau, 107 Lincoln St., Huntsville, AL 35801	256-533-1640	n/a	info@northalaba ma.bbb.org	www.northalabam a.bbb.org

STATE	ADDRESS	TELEPHONE	FAX	EMAIL	WEBSITE
Alabama	Better Business Bureau, 500 Eastern Boulevard, Ste.128, Montgomery, AL 36117	334-262-5606	334-273-5546	info@montgomery.bbb.org	n/a
Alaska	Better Business Bureau, 2805 Bering St. Suite 5, Anchorage, AK 99503-3819	907-562-0704	907-562-4061	alaskacb@gci.net	www.alaska.bbb.org
Arizona	Better Business Bureau, 4428 North 12th St., Phoenix, AZ 85014-4585	602-264-1721	602-263-0997	info@phoenix.bbb.org	www.phoenix.bbb.org
Arizona	Better Business Bureau, 3620 North 1st Ave., Suite 136, Tucson, AZ 85719	520-888-5353	520-888-6262	info@tucson.bbb.org	www.tucson.bbb.org

STATE	ADDRESS	TELEPHONE	FAX	EMAIL	WEBSITE
Arkansas	Better Business Bureau, 12521 Kanis Road, Little Rock, AR 72211	501-664-7274	501-664-0024	info@bbbarkansas.org	www.arkansas.-bbb.org
California	Better Business Bureau, 1601 H St., Suite 101, Bakersfield, CA 93301-1311	661-322-2074	661-322-8318	info@bbbfresno.org	www.cencal.bbb.org
California	Better Business Bureau, PO Box 970, Colton, CA 92324	909-835-6064	909-825-6246	info@la.bbb.org	www.bbbsouthland.org
California	Better Business Bureau, 315 North La Cadena Drive, Colton, CA 92324-0814	909-825-7280	909-825-6246	info@la.bbb.org	www.bbbsouthland.org
California	Better Business Bureau, 1 7609 Ventura Blvd. Ste LL03, Encino, CA 91316	818-836-5510	818-386-5513	info@encino.bbb.org	www.bbbsouthland.org

STATE	ADDRESS	TELEPHONE	FAX	EMAIL	WEBSITE
California	Better Business Bureau, 2519 West Shaw, #106, Fresno, CA 93711	559-222-8111	559-228-6518	info@bbbfresno.org	www.fresno.bbb.org
California	Better Business Bureau, 510 Broadway Suite 200, Millbrae, CA 94030	650-552-9222	650-652-1748	info@sanmateo.bbb.org	www.sanmateo.bbb.org
California	Better Business Bureau, 510 16th St., Suite 550, Oakland, CA 94612-1584	415-243-9999	510-238-1018	info@oakland.bbb.org	www.oakland.bbb.org
California	Better Business Bureau, 550 W. Orangethorpe Ave., Placentia, CA 92870	714-985-8922	714-985-8920	info@la.bbb.org	www.bbbsouthland.org

STATE	ADDRESS	TELEPHONE	FAX	EMAIL	WEBSITE
California	Better Business Bureau, 400 S St., Sacramento, CA 958146997	916-443-6843	916-441-3356	info@sacramento.bbb.org	www.sacramento.bbb.org
California	Better Business Bureau, 5050 Murphy Canyon, Ste. 110, San Diego, CA 92123	858-496-2131	858-496-2141	info@sandiego.bbb.org	www.sandiego.bbb.org
California	Better Business Bureau, 2100 Forest Ave. Suite 110, San Jose, CA 95128	408-278-7400	408-278-7444	info@bbbsilicon.org	www.bbbsilicon.org
California	Better Business Bureau, PO Box 129, Santa Barbara, CA 93102	805-963-8657	805-962-8557	info@santabarbara.bbb.org	www.santabarbara.bbb.org
California	Better Business Bureau, 11 S San Joaquin St, Suite 803, Stockton, CA 95202-3202	209-948-4880	209-465-6302	info@stockton.bbb.org	www.stockton.bbb.org

STATE	ADDRESS	TELEPHONE	FAX	EMAIL	WEBSITE
California	Better Business Bureau, 20280 S Vermont, Suite 201 Torrance, CA 90502	310-771-1447	310-771-1446	info@la.bbb.org	www.bbbsouthland .org
Colorado	Better Business Bureau, 25 North Wahsatch, Colorado Springs, CO 80903	719-636-1155	719-636-5078	info@colorado-springs.bbb.org	www.colorado-springs.bbb.org
Colorado	Better Business Bureau, 1780 South Bellaire, Suite 700 Denver, CO 80222-4350	303-758-2100	303-758-8321	info@denver.bbb.org	www.denver.bbb.org
Colorado	Better Business Bureau, 1730 South College Ave., Suite 303 Fort Collins, CO 80525	970-484-1348	970-221-1239	info@rockymtn.bbb.org	www.rockymtn.bbb.org

STATE	ADDRESS	TELEPHONE	FAX	EMAIL	WEBSITE
Colorado	Better Business Bureau, 119 West 6th St., Suite 203 Pueblo, CO 81003-3119	719-542-6464	719-542-5229	info@pueblo.bbb. org	www.pueblo.bbb. org
Connecticut	Better Business Bureau, 821 North Main St. Ext., Wallingford, CT 06492-2420	203-269-2700	203-269-3124	info@ctbbb.org	www.connecticut. bbb.org
Delaware	Better Business Bureau, 1010 Concord Ave., Suite 101, Wilmington, DE 19802	302-594-9200	302-594-1052	info@wilmington. bbb.org	www.wilmington. bbb.org
District of Columbia	Better Business Bureau, 1411 K St. NW, 10th Floor, Washington, DC 20005-3404	202-393-8000	202-393-1198	info@dc.bbb.org	www.dc.bbb.org

STATE	ADDRESS	TELEPHONE	FAX	EMAIL	WEBSITE
Florida	Better Business Bureau, 151 South Wymore Rd Suite 100, Altamonte Springs, FL 32714	407-621-3300	407-786-2625	info@orlando.bbb.org	www.orlando.bbb.org
Florida	Better Business Bureau, PO Box 7950, Clearwater, FL 337587950	727-535-5522	727-539-6301	clrwatcb@gte.net	www.clearwater.bbb.org
Florida	Better Business Bureau, 7820 Arlington Expressway, #147, Jacksonville, FL 32211	904-721-2288	904-721-7373	bbbnefla@bell-south.net	www.jacksonville.bbb.org
Florida	Better Business Bureau, 9050 Pines Blvd, Ste. 358, Pembroke Pines, FL 33024	954-431-4900	954-431-7509	westpalm@gte.net	www.bbbsouth-eastflorida.org

STATE	ADDRESS	TELEPHONE	FAX	EMAIL	WEBSITE
Florida	Better Business Bureau, PO Box 1511, Pensacola, FL 32597-1511	850-429-0002	850-429-0006	info@pensacola.bbb.org	www.pensacola.bbb.org
Florida	Better Business Bureau, 1950 SE Port St. Lucie Blvd. Suite 211, Port St. Lucie, FL 34952-5579	772-878-2010	772-335-9486	westpalm@gte.net	www.bbbsoutheastflorida.org
Florida	Better Business Bureau, 2924 N. Australian Ave., West Palm Beach, FL 33407	561-842-1918	561-845-7234	westpalm@gte.net	www.bbbsoutheastflorida.org
Georgia	Better Business Bureau, PO Box 161447, Atlanta, GA 30321	404-766-0875	404-768-1085	info@atlanta.bbb.org	www.atlanta.bbb.org
Georgia	Better Business Bureau, P.O. Box 2085, Augusta, GA 309032085	706-722-1574	706-724-0969	info@augusta-ga.bbb.org	www.augusta-ga.bbb.org

STATE	ADDRESS	TELEPHONE	FAX	EMAIL	WEBSITE
Georgia	Better Business Bureau, P.O. Box 2587, Columbus, GA 31902-2587	706-324-0712	706-324-2181	nfo@columbus-ga.bbb.org	www.columbus-ga.bbb.org
Georgia	Better Business Bureau, 277 Martin Luther King Jr Boulevard, Suite 102, Macon, GA 31201-3495	478-742-7999	478-742-8191	info@macon.bbb.org	www.macon.bbb.org
Georgia	Better Business Bureau, 6606 Abercorn St., Suite 108-C, Savannah, GA 31405-5817	912-354-7521	912-354-5068	bbbsea@bellsouth eastatlantic.org	www.bbbsouth-eastatlantic.org
Hawaii	Better Business Bureau, 1132 Bishop St., Suite 1507 Honolulu, HI 96813-2822	808-536-6956	808-523-2335	info@hawaii.bbb.org	www.hawaii.bbb.org
Idaho	Better Business Bureau, 4619 Emerald St., Suite A2, Boise, ID 83706	208-342-4649	208-342-5116	n/a	www.boise.bbb.org

STATE	ADDRESS	TELEPHONE	FAX	EMAIL	WEBSITE
Idaho	Better Business Bureau, 1575 South Blvd., Idaho Falls, ID 83404-5926	208-523-9754	208-524-6190	bbb-if@srv.net	www.idahofalls.bbb.org
Illinois	Better Business Bureau, 330 North Wabash Ave., Suite 2006 Chicago, IL 60611	312-832-0500	312-832-9985	feedback@chicago.bbb.org	www.chicago.bbb.org
Illinois	Better Business Bureau, 3024 West Lake Ave., Suite 200, Peoria, IL 61615-3770	309-688-3741	309-681-7290	bbb@heart.net	www.peoria.bbb.org
Illinois	Better Business Bureau, 810 East State St., 3rd Floor, Rockford, IL 61104-1001	815-963-2222	815-963-0329	feedback@chicago.bbb.org	www.chicago.bbb.org
Indiana	Better Business Bureau, PO Box 405, Elkhart, IN 46515-0405	219-423-4433	219-266-2026	info@fortwayne.bbb.org	www.elkhart.bbb.org

STATE	ADDRESS	TELEPHONE	FAX	EMAIL	WEBSITE
Indiana	Better Business Bureau, 1139 Washington Square, Evansville, IN 47715	812-473-0202	812-473-3080	info@evansville.bbb.org	www.evansville.bbb.org
Indiana	Better Business Bureau, 1203 Webster St., Fort Wayne, IN 46802-3493	219-423-4433	219-423-3301	info@fortwayne.bbb.org	www.fortwayne.bbb.org
Indiana	Better Business Bureau, 22 East Washington St., Suite 200, Victoria Center Indianapolis, IN 46204-3584	317-488-2222	317-488-2224	info@indybbb.org	www.indybbb.org
Indiana	Better Business Bureau, 6111 Harrison St., Suite 101, Merriville, IN 46410	219-980-1511	219-884-2123	info@nwin.bbb.org	www.gary.bbb.org

STATE	ADDRESS	TELEPHONE	FAX	EMAIL	WEBSITE
Indiana	Better Business Bureau, 207 Dixie Way North, Suite 130, South Bend, IN 46637-3360	219-277-9121	219-273-6666	info@nwin.bbb.org	n/a
Iowa	Better Business Bureau, 2435 Kimberly Rd, Suite 175N, Bettendorf, IA 52722-4100	319-355-6544	319-355-0306	info@dm.bbb.org	www.desmoines.bbb.org
Iowa	Better Business Bureau, 505 5th Ave., Suite 950, Des Moines, IA 50309-2375	515-243-8137	515-243-2227	info@dm.bbb.org	www.desmoines.bbb.org
Iowa	Better Business Bureau, 505 6th St., Suite 300, Sioux City, IA 51101	712-252-4501	712-252-0285	general@siouxland.bbb.org	www.siouxlandbbb.org

STATE	ADDRESS	TELEPHONE	FAX	EMAIL	WEBSITE
Kansas	Better Business Bureau, 501 Southeast Jefferson, Suite 24, Topeka, KS 66607-1190	785-232-9677	n/a	info@topeka.bbb.org	www.topeka.bbb.org
Kansas	Better Business Bureau, 328 Laura, Wichita, KS 67211	316-263-3146	316-263-3063	info@wichita.bbb.org	www.wichita.bbb.org
Kentucky	Better Business Bureau, 1460 Newtown Pike, Lexington, KY 40511	859-259-1008	859-259-1639	info@lexington.bbb.org	www.lexington.bbb.org
Kentucky	Better Business Bureau, 844 South Fourth St., Louisville, KY 40203-2186	502-583-6546	502-589-9940	business@ky-in.bbb.org	ww.ky-in.bbb.org
Louisiana	Better Business Bureau, 5220C Rue Verdun, Alexandria, LA 71303	318-473-4494	318-473-8906	info@alexandria-la.bbb.org	www.alexandria-la.bbb.org

STATE	ADDRESS	TELEPHONE	FAX	EMAIL	WEBSITE
Louisiana	Better Business Bureau, 748 Main St., Baton Rouge, LA 70802	225-346-5222	225-346-1029	info@batonrouge.bbb.org	www.batonrouge.bbb.org
Louisiana	Better Business Bureau, 5953 West Park Ave., Suite 4005 Houma, LA 70364	504-868-3456	5C4-876-7664	info@neworleans.bbb.org	www.houma.bbb.org
Louisiana	Better Business Bureau, 4007 West Congress St., Suite B, Lafayette, LA 70506	337-981-3497	337-981-7559	info@acadiana.bbb.org	www.acadiana.bbb.org
Louisiana	Better Business Bureau, PO Box 7314, Lake Charles, LA 70606-7314	337-478-6253	337-474-8981	info@lakecharles.bbb.org	www.lakecharles.bbb.org
Louisiana	Better Business Bureau, 141 Desiard St., Suite 808 Monroe, LA 71201-7345	318-387-4600	318-361-0461	monroe@gte.net	www.monroe.bbb.org

STATE	ADDRESS	TELEPHONE	FAX	EMAIL	WEBSITE
Louisiana	Better Business Bureau, 1539 Jackson Ave., Suite 400, New Orleans, LA	70130-5843	504-524-9110	info@neworleans. bbb.org	www.neworleans. bbb.org
Louisiana	Better Business Bureau, 3612 Youree Dr., Shreveport, LA 71105-2122	318-868-5146	318-861-6426	info@shreveport. bbb.org	www.shreveport. bbb.org
Maine	Better Business Bureau, 812 Stevens Ave., Portland, ME 041032648	207-878-2715	207-797-5818	info@bosbbb.org	www.bosbbb.org
Maryland	Better Business Bureau, 2100 Huntingdon Ave., Baltimore, MD 21211-3215	410-347-3990	410-347-3936	info@bbbmd.org	www.baltimore. bbb.org
Massachusetts	Better Business Bureau, 235 West Central St., Suite 1, Natick, MA 01760	508-652-4800	508-652-4833	info@bosbbb.org	www.bosbbb.org

STATE	ADDRESS	TELEPHONE	FAX	EMAIL	WEBSITE
Massachusetts	Better Business Bureau, 293 Bridge St., Suite 409, Springfield, MA 01103-1402	413-734-3114	413-734-2006	info@springfield-ma.bbb.org	www.springfield-ma.bbb.org
Massachusetts	Better Business Bureau, PO Box 16555, Worcester, MA 01601-6555	508-755-2548	508-754-4158	info@wooster.bbb.org	www.worcester.bbb.org
Michigan	Better Business Bureau, 40 Pearl, NW, Suite 354, Grand Rapids, MI 49503	616-774-8236	616—774-2014	bbbinfo@iserv.net	www.grandrapids.bbb.org
Michigan	Better Business Bureau, 30555 Southfield Road, Suite 200, Southfield, MI 48076-7751	248-644-9100	248-644-5026	info@easternmi-chiganbbb.org	www.easternmi-chiganbbb.org
Minnesota	Better Business Bureau, 2706 Gannon Road, St. Paul, MN 55116-2600	651-699-1111	651-699-7665	ask@mnd.bbb.org	www.mnd.bbb.org

STATE	ADDRESS	TELEPHONE	FAX	EMAIL	WEBSITE
Mississippi	Better Business Bureau, PO Box 12745, Jackson, MS 39236-2745	601-987-8282	601-987-8285	info@bbbmississippi.org	www.bbbmississippi.org
Missouri	Better Business Bureau, 8080 Ward Parkway, Suite 200, Kansas City, MO 64114	816-421-7800	816-472-5442	info@kansascitybbb.org	www.kansascity.bbb.org
Missouri	Better Business Bureau, 205 Park Central East, Suite 509, Springfield, MO 65806-1326	417-862-4222	417-869-5544	info@springfieldmo.bbb.org	www.springfieldmo.bbb.org
Missouri	Better Business Bureau, 12 Sunnen Dr., Suite 121, St. Louis, MO 63143	314-645-3300	314-645-2666	bbbstl@stlouisbbb.org	www.stlouis.bbb.org
Nebraska	Better Business Bureau, 3633 O St., Suite 1, Lincoln, NE 68510-1670	402-436-2345	402-476-8221	info@lincoln.bbb.org	www.lincoln.bbb.org

STATE	ADDRESS	TELEPHONE	FAX	EMAIL	WEBSITE
Nebraska	Better Business Bureau, 2237 North 91st Court, Omaha, NE 68134-6022	402-391-7612	402-391-7535	info@heartlandbbb.org	www.heartlandbbb.org
Nevada	Better Business Bureau, 2301 Palomino Lane, Las Vegas, NV 89107	702-320-4500	702-320-4560	scampbell@vegasbbb.org	www.vegasbbb.org
Nevada	Better Business Bureau, PO Box 21269, Reno, NV 89515-1269	775-322-0657	775-322-3163	information@renobbb.org	www.reno.bbb.org
New Hampshire	Better Business Bureau, 410 South Main St., Concord, NH 03301-3483	603-224-1991	603-228-9035	bbb@conknet.com	www.concord.bbb.org
New Jersey	Better Business Bureau, 400 Lanidex Plaza, Parsippany, NJ 07054-2797	973-581-1616	973-581-7022	bbb.nj@att.net	www.parsippany.bbb.org

STATE	ADDRESS	TELEPHONE	FAX	EMAIL	WEBSITE
New Jersey	Better Business Bureau, 1721 Route 37 East, Toms River, NJ 08753-8239	732-270-5577	732-270-8739	info@trenton.bbb. org	www.trenton.bbb. org
New Jersey	Better Business Bureau, 1700 Whitehorse-Hamilton Square, Suite D-5, Trenton, NJ 08690-3596	609-588-0808	609-588-0546	info@trenton.bbb. org	www.trenton.bbb. org
New Mexico	Better Business Bureau, 2625 Pennsylvania, NE, Ste 2050, Albuquerque, NM 87110-3657	505-346-0110	505-346-0696	bureau@bbbnm. com	www.bbbnm.com
New Mexico	Better Business Bureau, 308 North Locke, Farmington, NM 87401-5855	505-326-6502	505-327-7731	info@farmington. bbb.org	www.farmington. bbb.org

STATE	ADDRESS	TELEPHONE	FAX	EMAIL	WEBSITE
New York	Better Business Bureau, 741 Delaware, Suite 100, Buffalo, NY 14209-2201	716-881-5222	716-833-5349	info@upstatenybbb.org	www.upstateny.bbb.org
New York	Better Business Bureau, 266 Main St., Farmingdale, NY 11735-2618	212-553-6200	516-420-1095	longisland@newyork.bbb.org	www.newyork.bbb.org
New York	Better Business Bureau, 257 Park Ave. South, New York, NY 10010-7384	212-553-6200	212-477-4912	bbb@bway.net	www.newyork.bbb.org
New York	Better Business Bureau, 55 St. Paul St., Rochester, NY 14604	716-881-5222	n/a	n/a	www.rcchester.bbb.org
New York	Better Business Bureau, 1153 W. Fayette, Suite 300, Syracuse, NY 13204	716-881-5222	315-475-0769	dpalm@upstateny.bbb.org	www.syracuse.bbb.org

STATE	ADDRESS	TELEPHONE	FAX	EMAIL	WEBSITE
New York	Better Business Bureau, 30 Glenn St., White Plains, NY 10603-3213	212-533-6200	914-428-6030	mhbbb@westnet. com	www.newyork.bbb. org
North Carolina	Better Business Bureau, One West Pack Sq., Ste 1601, Asheville, NC 28801-3408	828-253-2392	828-252-5039	info@asheville.bbb. org	www.asheville.bbb. org
North Carolina	Better Business Bureau, 5200 Park Road, Suite 202, Charlotte, NC 28209	704-527-0012	704-525-7624	info@charlotte. bbb.org	www.charlotte. bbb.org
North Carolina	Better Business Bureau, 106-A Bradfoot Ave, Fayetteville, NC 28305	910-436-1473	910-486-6229	n/a	www.carolina.bbb. org
North Carolina	Better Business Bureau, 3608 West Friendly Ave., Greensboro, NC 27410-4895	336-852-4240	336-852-7540	info@greensboro. bbb.org	www.greensboro. bbb.org

STATE	ADDRESS	TELEPHONE	FAX	EMAIL	WEBSITE
North Carolina	Better Business Bureau, 5540 Munford Road, Suite 130, Raleigh, NC 27612	919-277-4222	919-277-4221	info@raleigh.bbb. org	www.bbbenc.org
North Carolina	Better Business Bureau, 500 West 5th St., Suite 202, Winston-Salem, NC 27101-2728	336-725-8348	336-777-3727	bbb@nwncbbb. com	www.winston-salem.bbb.org
Ohio	Better Business Bureau, 222 West Market St., Akron, OH 44303	330-253-4590	330-253-6249	info@akron.bbb. org	www.akronbbb. org
Ohio	Better Business Bureau, PO Box 8017, Canton, OH 44711-8017	330-454-9401	330-456-8957	info@cantonbbb. org	www.cantonbbb. org
Ohio	Better Business Bureau, 898 Walnut St., Cincinnati, OH 45202-2097	513-421-3015	513-621-0907	info@cincinnati. bbb.org	www.cinbbb.org

STATE	ADDRESS	TELEPHONE	FAX	EMAIL	WEBSITE
Ohio	Better Business Bureau, 2217 East 9th St., Suite 200, Cleveland, OH 44115-1299	216-241-7678	216-861-6365	info@cleveland.bbb.org	www.cleveland.bbb.org
Ohio	Better Business Bureau, 1335 Dublin Road, Suite 30 A, Columbus, OH 43215-1000	614-486-6336	614-486-6631	info@columbus-ohbbb.org	www.columbus-ohbbb.org
Ohio	Better Business Bureau, 40 West Fourth St., Suite 1250, Dayton, OH 45402-1830	937-222-5825	937-222-3338	info@dayton.bbb.org	www.dayton.bbb.org
Ohio	Better Business Bureau, PO Box 269, Lima, OH 45801	419-223-7010	419-229-2029	info@bbbwco.org	www.wcohio.bbb.org

STATE	ADDRESS	TELEPHONE	FAX	EMAIL	WEBSITE
Ohio	Better Business Bureau, 3103 Executive Parkway, Suite 200 Toledo, OH 43606-1310	419-531-3116	419-578-6001	info@toledobbb. org	www.toledo.bbb. org
Ohio	Better Business Bureau, PO Box 1495, Youngstown, OH 44503	330-394-0628	330-744-7536	info@youngstown bbb.org	www.youngstown bbb.org
Oklahoma	Better Business Bureau, 17 South Dewey Ave., Oklahoma City, OK 73102-2400	405-239-6081	405-235-5891	info@oklahoma city.bbb.org	www.oklahoma city.bbb.org
Oklahoma	Better Business Bureau, 4530 S. Sheridan, Ste. 218, Tulsa, OK 74145	918-492-1266	918-492-1276	info@tulsabbb. org	www.tulsabbb.org

STATE	ADDRESS	TELEPHONE	FAX	EMAIL	WEBSITE
Oregon	Better Business Bureau, 333 SW Fifth Ave., Suite 300, Portland, OR 97204	503-226-3981	503-226-8200	info@wwbbb.org	www.orwwabbb.org
Pennsylvania	Better Business Bureau, 528 North New St., Bethlehem, PA 18018-5789	610-866-8780	610-868-8668	bethlehem@easternpa.bbb.org	www.easternpa.bbb.org
Pennsylvania	Better Business Bureau, 29 East King St. Suite 322, Lancaster, PA 17602-2852	717-291-1151	717-291-3241	lancaster@easternpa.bbb.org	www.easternpa.bbb.org
Pennsylvania	Better Business Bureau, 4099 Birney Avenue, Moosic, PA 18507	570-342-5714	570-342-1282	info@nepa.bbb.org	www.nepa.bbb.org
Pennsylvania	Better Business Bureau, 1608 Walnut St., Suite 402 Philadelphia, PA 19103-0297	215-985-9313	215-893-9312	philadelphia@easternpa.bbb.org	www.easternpa.bbb.org

STATE	ADDRESS	TELEPHONE	FAX	EMAIL	WEBSITE
Pennsylvania	Better Business Bureau, 300 Sixth Ave., Ste 100-UL, Pittsburgh, PA 15222-2511	412-456-2700	412-456-2739	info@pittsburgh. bbb.org	www.pittsburgh. bbb.org
Puerto Rico	Better Business Bureau, PO Box 363488, San Juan, PR 00936-3488	787-756-5400	787-758-0095	info@sanjuan. bbb.org	n/a
Rhode Island	Better Business Bureau, 120 Lavan St., Warwick, RI 028881071	401-785-1212	410-785-3061	info@rhodeisland. bbb.org	www.rhodeisland. bbb.org
South Carolina	Better Business Bureau, PO Box 8326, Columbia, SC 29202	803-254-2525	803-779-3117	info@columbia. bbb.org	www.columbia. bbb.org
South Carolina	Better Business Bureau, 307-B Falls St., Greenville, SC 29601-2829	864-242-5052	864-271-9802	info@greenville. bbb.org	www.greenville. bbb.org

STATE	ADDRESS	TELEPHONE	FAX	EMAIL	WEBSITE
South Carolina	Better Business Bureau, 1601 North Oak St., Suite 101 Myrtle Beach, SC 29577-1601	843-626-6881	843-626-7455	mrtlebcb@gte.net	www.carolina.bbb.org
Tennessee	Better Business Bureau, PO Box 1178, Blountville, TN 37617-1178	423-325-6616	423-325-6621	info@knoxville.bbb.org	www.knoxville.bbb.org
Tennessee	Better Business Bureau, 1010 Market St., Suite 200, Chattanooga, TN 37402-2614	423-266-6144	423-267-1924	tngabbb@gte.net	www.chattanooga.bbb.org
Tennessee	Better Business Bureau, PO Box 1456, Clarksville, TN 37041	931-503-2222	931-503-2234	bbbclarks@aol.com	www.middleten-nessee.bbb.org
Tennessee	Better Business Bureau, 206 E College St., Fayetteville, TN 37334	931-433-9501	931-433-7424	bbbfayette@aol.com	www.middleten-nessee.bbb.org

STATE	ADDRESS	TELEPHONE	FAX	EMAIL	WEBSITE
Tennessee	Better Business Bureau, PO Box 31377, Knoxville, TN 37930	865-692-1600	865-692-1590	info@knoxville. bbb.org	www.knoxville. bbb.org
Tennessee	Better Business Bureau, PO Box 17036, Memphis, TN 38120	901-759-1300	901-757-2997	info@bbbmidsouth .org	www.midsouth. bbb.org
Tennessee	Better Business Bureau, 1231 NW Broad St., Murfreesboro, TN 37129	615-242-4222	615-867-3905	bbbmurf@aol.com	www.middleten-nessee.bbb.org
Tennessee	Better Business Bureau, PO Box 198436, Nashville, TN 37219-8436	615-250-4222	615-250-4245	bbbnash@aol.com	www.middleten-nessee.bbb.org
Texas	Better Business Bureau, 3300 South 14th St., Suite 307, Abilene, TX 79605-5052	915-691-1533	915-691-0309	info@abilene.bbb. org	www.abilene.bbb. org

STATE	ADDRESS	TELEPHONE	FAX	EMAIL	WEBSITE
Texas	Better Business Bureau, PO Box 1905, Amarillo, TX 79105-3905	806-379-6222	806-379-8206	info@amarillo. bbb.org	www.amarillo.bbb. org
Texas	Better Business Bureau, 2101 South IH35, Suite 302, Austin, TX 78741-3854	512-445-2911	512-445-2096	info@austin.bbb. org	www.centraltx. bbb.org
Texas	Better Business Bureau, PO Box 2988, Beaumont, TX 77704-2988	409-835-5348	409-838-6858	bureau@bbbse texas.org	www.bbbsetexas. org
Texas	Better Business Bureau, PO Box 3868, Bryan, TX 77805-3868	979-260-2222	979-846-0276	info@bbbbryan. org	www.bryan.bbb. org
Texas	Better Business Bureau, 4301 Ocean Dr., Corpus Christi, TX 78412	361-852-4949	361-852-4990	info@corpuschristi .bbb.org	www.caller.com/ bbb

STATE	ADDRESS	TELEPHONE	FAX	EMAIL	WEBSITE
Texas	Better Business Bureau, 1600 Pacific Suite 2800, Dallas, TX 75201-5093	214-220-2000	214-740-0321	info@dallas.bbb.org	www.dallas.bbb.org
Texas	Better Business Bureau, 221 N. Kansas, Suite 1101, El Paso, TX 79901	915-577-0191	915-577-0209	n/a	www.bbbelpaso.com
Texas	Better Business Bureau, 1612 Summit Ave., Suite 260, Fort Worth, TX 76102-5978	817-332-7585	817-382-0566	bbb@fwbbb.org	www.fortworth.bbb.org
Texas	Better Business Bureau, 5225 Katy Freeway, Suite 500, Houston, TX 77007	713-868-9500	713-341-6142	bbbinfo@bbbhou.org	www.bbbhou.org

STATE	ADDRESS	TELEPHONE	FAX	EMAIL	WEBSITE
Texas	Better Business Bureau, 1125 Judson Road, Suite 114, Longview, TX 75601	903-758-3222	903-758-3226	n/a	n/a
Texas	Better Business Bureau, 3333 66th St., Lubbock, TX 79413-5711	806-763-0459	806-744-9748	info@bbbsouthpla ins.org	www.bbbsouthpla ins.org
Texas	Better Business Bureau, PO Box 60206, Midland, TX 79706	915-563-1880	915-561-9435	info@bbbpb.org	www.midland.bbb. org
Texas	Better Business Bureau, PO Box 3366, San Angelo, TX 76902-3366	915-949-2989	915-949-3514	sanangcb@gte.net	www.sanangelo. bbb.org
Texas	Better Business Bureau, 1800 Northeast Loop, 410, Suite 400, San Antonio, TX 78217-5296	210-828-9441	210-828-3101	info@sanantonio. bbb.org	www.sanantonio. bbb.org

STATE	ADDRESS	TELEPHONE	FAX	EMAIL	WEBSITE
Texas	Better Business Bureau, PO Box 6652, Tyler, TX 75711	903-581-5704	903-534-8644	contactus@tyler.bbb.org	www.tyler.bbb.org
Texas	Better Business Bureau, 2210 Washington Ave., Waco, TX 76701-1019	254-755-7772	254-755-7774	info@waco.bbb.org	www.waco.bbb.org
Texas	Better Business Bureau, PO Box 69, Weslaco, TX 78599-0069	956-968-3678	956-968-7638	n/a	www.weslaco.bbb.org
Texas	Better Business Bureau, 4245 Kemp Blvd., Suite 900, Wichita Falls TX 76308-2830	940-691-1172	940-691-1175	info@bbbnorcentx.org	www.bbbnorcentx.org
Utah	Better Business Bureau, 5673 S. Redwood Rd., Suite 22, Taylorsville, UT 84123-5322	801-892-6009	801-892-6002	info@utah.bbb.org	www.saltlakecity.bbb.org

STATE	ADDRESS	TELEPHONE	FAX	EMAIL	WEBSITE
Virginia	Better Business Bureau, 4200 Wilson Blvd Suite 800, Arlington, VA 22203-1838	703-525-8277	n/a	n/a	www.bbb.org
Virginia	Better Business Bureau, 586 Virginian Dr., Norfolk, VA 23505	757-531-1300	757-531-1388	info@hampton-roadsbbb.org	www.norfolk.bbb.org
Virginia	Better Business Bureau, 701 East Franklin, Suite 712, Richmond, VA 23219-2332	804-648-0016	804-648-3115	info@richmond.bbb.org	www.richmond.bbb.org
Virginia	Better Business Bureau, 31 West Campbell Ave., Roanoke, VA 24011-1301	540-342-3455	540-345-2289	info@roanoke.va bbb.org	www.vabbb.org
Washington	Better Business Bureau, 101 North Union, #105, Kennewick, WA 99336-3819	509-783-0892	509-783-2893	info@thelocalbbb.org	www.thelocalbbb.org

STATE	ADDRESS	TELEPHONE	FAX	EMAIL	WEBSITE
Washington	Better Business Bureau, PO Box 68926, Sea Tac, WA 98168-0926	206-431-2222	206-431-2211	info@wwbbb.org	www.orwwa.bbb.org
Washington	Better Business Bureau, 508 West 6th Ave., Suite 401, Spokane, WA 99204-2356	509-455-4200	509-838-1079	info@thelocalbbb.org	www.thelocalbbb.org
West Virginia	Better Business Bureau, PO Box 2541, Charleston, WV 25329-9903	304-345-75C2	304-345-7511	info@cantonbbb.org	www.westvirginiabbb.org
Wisconsin	Better Business Bureau, PO Box 2190, Milwaukee, WI 53201	414-847-6000	414-3C2-0355	info@wisconsin.bbb.org	www.wisconsin.bbb.org

Source: Federal Citizen Information Center U.S. General Services Administration.

APPENDIX 11:
MAGNUSSON MOSS WARRANTY ACT

SEC. 2301. —DEFINITIONS

For the purposes of this chapter:

(1) The term "consumer product" means any tangible personal property which is distributed in commerce and which is normally used for personal, family, or household purposes (including any such property intended to be attached to or installed in any real property without regard to whether it is so attached or installed).

(2) The term "Commission" means the Federal Trade Commission.

(3) The term "consumer" means a buyer (other than for purposes of resale) of any consumer product, any person to whom such product is transferred during the duration of an implied or written warranty (or service contract) applicable to the product, and any other person who is entitled by the terms of such warranty (or service contract) or under applicable State law to enforce against the warrantor (or service contractor) the obligations of the warranty (or service contract).

(4) The term "supplier" means any person engaged in the business of making a consumer product directly or indirectly available to consumers.

(5) The term "warrantor" means any supplier or other person who gives or offers to give a written warranty or who is or may be obligated under an implied warranty.

(6) The term "written warranty" means—

(A) any written affirmation of fact or written promise made in connection with the sale of a consumer product by a supplier to a buyer which relates to the nature of the material or workmanship and affirms or promises that such material or workmanship is defect free or will meet a specified level of performance over a specified period of time, or

(B) any undertaking in writing in connection with the sale by a supplier of a consumer product to refund, repair, replace, or take other remedial action with respect to such product in the event that such product fails to meet the specifications set forth in the undertaking, which written affirmation, promise, or undertaking becomes part of the basis of the bargain between a supplier and a buyer for purposes other than resale of such product.

(7) The term "implied warranty" means an implied warranty arising under State law (as modified by sections 2308 and 2304(a) of this title) in connection with the sale by a supplier of a consumer product.

(8) The term "service contract" means a contract in writing to perform, over a fixed period of time or for a specified duration, services relating to the maintenance or repair (or both) of a consumer product.

(9) The term "reasonable and necessary maintenance" consists of those operations

(A) which the consumer reasonably can be expected to perform or have performed and

(B) which are necessary to keep any consumer product performing its intended function and operating at a reasonable level of performance.

(10) The term "remedy" means whichever of the following actions the warrantor elects:

(A) repair,

(B) replacement, or

(C) refund; except that the warrantor may not elect refund unless

(i) the warrantor is unable to provide replacement and repair is not commercially practicable or cannot be timely made, or

(ii) the consumer is willing to accept such refund.

(11) The term "replacement" means furnishing a new consumer product which is identical or reasonably equivalent to the warranted consumer product.

(12) The term "refund" means refunding the actual purchase price (less reasonable depreciation based on actual use where permitted by rules of the Commission).

(13) The term "distributed in commerce" means sold in commerce, introduced or delivered for introduction into commerce, or held for sale or distribution after introduction into commerce.

(14) The term "commerce" means trade, traffic, commerce, or transportation—

(A) between a place in a State and any place outside thereof, or

(B) which affects trade, traffic, commerce, or transportation described in subparagraph (A).

(15) The term "State" means a State, the District of Columbia, the Commonwealth of Puerto Rico, the Virgin Islands, Guam, the Canal Zone, or American Samoa. The term "State law" includes a law of the United States applicable only to the District of Columbia or only to a territory or possession of the United States; and the term "Federal law" excludes any State law.

SEC. 2302.—RULES GOVERNING CONTENTS OF WARRANTIES

(a) Full and conspicuous disclosure of terms and conditions; additional requirements for contents

In order to improve the adequacy of information available to consumers, prevent deception, and improve competition in the marketing of consumer products, any warrantor warranting a consumer product to a consumer by means of a written warranty shall, to the extent required by rules of the Commission, fully and conspicuously disclose in simple and readily understood language the terms and conditions of such warranty. Such rules may require inclusion in the written warranty of any of the following items among others:

(1) The clear identification of the names and addresses of the warrantors.

(2) The identity of the party or parties to whom the warranty is extended.

(3) The products or parts covered.

(4) A statement of what the warrantor will do in the event of a defect, malfunction, or failure to conform with such written warranty—at whose expense—and for what period of time.

(5) A statement of what the consumer must do and expenses he must bear.

(6) Exceptions and exclusions from the terms of the warranty.

(7) The step-by-step procedure which the consumer should take in order to obtain performance of any obligation under the warranty,

including the identification of any person or class of persons authorized to perform the obligations set forth in the warranty.

(8) Information respecting the availability of any informal dispute settlement procedure offered by the warrantor and a recital, where the warranty so provides, that the purchaser may be required to resort to such procedure before pursuing any legal remedies in the courts.

(9) A brief, general description of the legal remedies available to the consumer.

(10) The time at which the warrantor will perform any obligations under the warranty.

(11) The period of time within which, after notice of a defect, malfunction, or failure to conform with the warranty, the warrantor will perform any obligations under the warranty.

(12) The characteristics or properties of the products, or parts thereof, that are not covered by the warranty.

(13) The elements of the warranty in words or phrases which would not mislead a reasonable, average consumer as to the nature or scope of the warranty.

(b) Availability of terms to consumer; manner and form for presentation and display of information; duration; extension of period for written warranty or service contract

(1)(A) The Commission shall prescribe rules requiring that the terms of any written warranty on a consumer product be made available to the consumer (or prospective consumer) prior to the sale of the product to him.

(1)(B) The Commission may prescribe rules for determining the manner and form in which information with respect to any written warranty of a consumer product shall be clearly and conspicuously presented or displayed so as not to mislead the reasonable, average consumer, when such information is contained in advertising, labeling, point-of-sale material, or other representations in writing.

(2) Nothing in this chapter (other than paragraph (3) of this subsection) shall be deemed to authorize the Commission to prescribe the duration of written warranties given or to require that a consumer product or any of its components be warranted.

(3) The Commission may prescribe rules for extending the period of time a written warranty or service contract is in effect to correspond with any period of time in excess of a reasonable period (not less than 10 days) during which the consumer is deprived of the use of such consumer product by reason of failure of the product to conform with

the written warranty or by reason of the failure of the warrantor (or service contractor) to carry out such warranty (or service contract) within the period specified in the warranty (or service contract).

(c) Prohibition on conditions for written or implied warranty; waiver by Commission

No warrantor of a consumer product may condition his written or implied warranty of such product on the consumer's using, in connection with such product, any article or service (other than article or service provided without charge under the terms of the warranty) which is identified by brand, trade, or corporate name; except that the prohibition of this subsection may be waived by the Commission if—

(1) the warrantor satisfies the Commission that the warranted product will function properly only if the article or service so identified is used in connection with the warranted product, and

(2) the Commission finds that such a waiver is in the public interest.

The Commission shall identify in the Federal Register, and permit public comment on, all applications for waiver of the prohibition of this subsection, and shall publish in the Federal Register its disposition of any such application, including the reasons therefor.

(d) Incorporation by reference of detailed substantive warranty provisions

The Commission may by rule devise detailed substantive warranty provisions which warrantors may incorporate by reference in their warranties.

(e) Applicability to consumer products costing more than $5

The provisions of this section apply only to warranties which pertain to consumer products actually costing the consumer more than $5.

SEC. 2303.—DESIGNATION OF WRITTEN WARRANTIES

(a) Full (statement of duration) or limited warranty

Any warrantor warranting a consumer product by means of a written warranty shall clearly and conspicuously designate such warranty in the following manner, unless exempted from doing so by the Commission pursuant to subsection (c) of this section:

(1) If the written warranty meets the Federal minimum standards for warranty set forth in section 2304 of this title, then it shall be conspicuously designated a "full (statement of duration) warranty".

(2) If the written warranty does not meet the Federal minimum standards for warranty set forth in section 2304 of this title, then it shall be conspicuously designated a "limited warranty".

(b) Applicability of requirements, standards, etc., to representations or statements of customer satisfaction

This section and sections 2302 and 2304 of this title shall not apply to statements or representations which are similar to expressions of general policy concerning customer satisfaction and which are not subject to any specific limitations.

(c) Exemptions by Commission

In addition to exercising the authority pertaining to disclosure granted in section 2302 of this title, the Commission may by rule determine when a written warranty does not have to be designated either "full (statement of duration)" or "limited" in accordance with this section.

(d) Applicability to consumer products costing more than $10 and not designated as full warranties

The provisions of subsections (a) and (c) of this section apply only to warranties which pertain to consumer products actually costing the consumer more than $10 and which are not designated "full (statement of duration) warranties."

SEC. 2304.—FEDERAL MINIMUM STANDARDS FOR WARRANTIES

(a) Remedies under written warranty; duration of implied warranty; exclusion or limitation on consequential damages for breach of written or implied warranty; election of refund or replacement

In order for a warrantor warranting a consumer product by means of a written warranty to meet the Federal minimum standards for warranty—

(1) such warrantor must as a minimum remedy such consumer product within a reasonable time and without charge, in the case of a defect, malfunction, or failure to conform with such written warranty;

(2) notwithstanding section 2308(b) of this title, such warrantor may not impose any limitation on the duration of any implied warranty on the product;

(3) such warrantor may not exclude or limit consequential damages for breach of any written or implied warranty on such product, unless such exclusion or limitation conspicuously appears on the face of the warranty; and

(4) if the product (or a component part thereof) contains a defect or malfunction after a reasonable number of attempts by the warrantor

to remedy defects or malfunctions in such product, such warrantor must permit the consumer to elect either a refund for, or replacement without charge of, such product or part (as the case may be). The Commission may by rule specify for purposes of this paragraph, what constitutes a reasonable number of attempts to remedy particular kinds of defects or malfunctions under different circumstances. If the warrantor replaces a component part of a consumer product, such replacement shall include installing the part in the product without charge.

(b) Duties and conditions imposed on consumer by warrantor

(1) In fulfilling the duties under subsection (a) of this section respecting a written warranty, the warrantor shall not impose any duty other than notification upon any consumer as a condition of securing remedy of any consumer product which malfunctions, is defective, or does not conform to the written warranty, unless the warrantor has demonstrated in a rulemaking proceeding, or can demonstrate in an administrative or judicial enforcement proceeding (including private enforcement), or in an informal dispute settlement proceeding, that such a duty is reasonable.

(2) Notwithstanding paragraph (1), a warrantor may require, as a condition to replacement of, or refund for, any consumer product under subsection (a) of this section, that such consumer product shall be made available to the warrantor free and clear of liens and other encumbrances, except as otherwise provided by rule or order of the Commission in cases in which such a requirement would not be practicable.

(3) The Commission may, by rule define in detail the duties set forth in subsection (a) of this section and the applicability of such duties to warrantors of different categories of consumer products with "full (statement of duration)" warranties.

(4) The duties under subsection (a) of this section extend from the warrantor to each person who is a consumer with respect to the consumer product.

(c) Waiver of standards

The performance of the duties under subsection (a) of this section shall not be required of the warrantor if he can show that the defect, malfunction, or failure of any warranted consumer product to conform with a written warranty, was caused by damage (not resulting from defect or malfunction) while in the possession of the consumer, or unreasonable use (including failure to provide reasonable and necessary maintenance).

(d) Remedy without charge

For purposes of this section and of section 2302(c) of this title, the term "without charge" means that the warrantor may not assess the consumer for any costs the warrantor or his representatives incur in connection with the required remedy of a warranted consumer product. An obligation under subsection (a)(1)(A) of this section to remedy without charge does not necessarily require the warrantor to compensate the consumer for incidental expenses; however, if any incidental expenses are incurred because the remedy is not made within a reasonable time or because the warrantor imposed an unreasonable duty upon the consumer as a condition of securing remedy, then the consumer shall be entitled to recover reasonable incidental expenses which are so incurred in any action against the warrantor.

(e) Incorporation of standards to products designated with full warranty for purposes of judicial actions

If a supplier designates a warranty applicable to a consumer product as a "full (statement of duration)" warranty, then the warranty on such product shall, for purposes of any action under section 2310(d) of this title or under any State law, be deemed to incorporate at least the minimum requirements of this section and rules prescribed under this section.

SEC. 2305.—FULL AND LIMITED WARRANTING OF A CONSUMER PRODUCT

Nothing in this chapter shall prohibit the selling of a consumer product which has both full and limited warranties if such warranties are clearly and conspicuously differentiated

SEC. 2306.—SERVICE CONTRACTS; RULES FOR FULL, CLEAR AND CONSPICUOUS DISCLOSURE OF TERMS AND CONDITIONS; ADDITION TO OR IN LIEU OF WRITTEN WARRANTY

(a) The Commission may prescribe by rule the manner and form in which the terms and conditions of service contracts shall be fully, clearly, and conspicuously disclosed.

(b) Nothing in this chapter shall be construed to prevent a supplier or warrantor from entering into a service contract with the consumer in addition to or in lieu of a written warranty if such contract fully, clearly, and conspicuously discloses its terms and conditions in simple and readily understood language.

SEC. 2307.—DESIGNATION OF REPRESENTATIVES BY WARRANTOR TO PERFORM DUTIES UNDER WRITTEN OR IMPLIED WARRANTY

Nothing in this chapter shall be construed to prevent any warrantor from designating representatives to perform duties under the written or implied warranty: Provided, That such warrantor shall make reasonable arrangements for compensation of such designated representatives, but no such designation shall relieve the warrantor of his direct responsibilities to the consumer or make the representative a cowarrantor.

SEC. 2308.—IMPLIED WARRANTIES

(a) Restrictions on disclaimers or modifications

No supplier may disclaim or modify (except as provided in subsection (b) of this section) any implied warranty to a consumer with respect to such consumer product if—

(1) such supplier makes any written warranty to the consumer with respect to such consumer Product, or

(2) at the time of sale, or within 90 days thereafter, such supplier enters into a service contract with the consumer which applies to such consumer product.

(b) Limitation on duration

For purposes of this chapter (other than section 2304(a)(2) of this title), implied warranties may be limited in duration to the duration of a written warranty of reasonable duration, if such limitation is conscionable and is set forth in clear and unmistakable language and prominently displayed on the face of the warranty.

(c) Effectiveness of disclaimers, modifications, or limitations

A disclaimer, modification, or limitation made in violation of this section shall be ineffective for purposes of this chapter and State law.

SEC. 2309.—PROCEDURES APPLICABLE TO PROMULGATION OF RULES BY COMMISSION

(a) Oral presentation

Any rule prescribed under this chapter shall be prescribed in accordance with section 553 of title 5; except that the Commission shall give interested persons an opportunity for oral presentations of data, views, and arguments, in addition to written submissions. A transcript shall be kept of any oral presentation. Any such rule shall be subject to judicial review under section 57a(e) of this title in the same manner as rules prescribed under section 57a(a)(1)(B) of this title, except that section 57a(e)(3)(B) of this title shall not apply.

(b) Warranties and warranty practices involved in sale of used motor vehicles

The Commission shall initiate within one year after January 4, 1975, a rulemaking proceeding dealing with warranties and warranty practices in connection with the sale of used motor vehicles; and, to the extent necessary to supplement the protections offered the consumer by this chapter, shall prescribe rules dealing with such warranties and practices. In prescribing rules under this subsection, the Commission may exercise any authority it may have under this chapter, or other law, and in addition it may require disclosure that a used motor vehicle is sold without any warranty and specify the form and content of such disclosure.

Sec. 2310.—Remedies in consumer disputes

(a) Informal dispute settlement procedures; establishment; rules setting forth minimum requirements; effect of compliance by warrantor; review of informal procedures or implementation by Commission; application to existing informal procedures

(1) Congress hereby declares it to be its policy to encourage warrantors to establish procedures whereby consumer disputes are fairly and expeditiously settled through informal dispute settlement mechanisms.

(2) The Commission shall prescribe rules setting forth minimum requirements for any informal dispute settlement procedure which is incorporated into the terms of a written warranty to which any provision of this chapter applies. Such rules shall provide for participation in such procedure by independent or governmental entities.

(3) One or more warrantors may establish an informal dispute settlement procedure which meets the requirements of the Commission's rules under paragraph (2). If—

(A) a warrantor establishes such a procedure,

(B) such procedure, and its implementation, meets the requirements of such rules, and

(C) he incorporates in a written warranty a requirement that the consumer resort to such procedure before pursuing any legal remedy under this section respecting such warranty, then

(i) the consumer may not commence a civil action (other than a class action) under subsection (d) of this section unless he initially resorts to such procedure; and

(ii) a class of consumers may not proceed in a class action under subsection (d) of this section except to the extent the court determines necessary to establish the representative capacity of the named plaintiffs, unless the named plaintiffs (upon notifying the defendant that they are named plaintiffs in a class action with respect to a warranty obligation) initially resort to such procedure. In the case of such a class action which is brought in a district court of the United States, the representative capacity of the named plaintiffs shall be established in the application of rule 23 of the Federal Rules of Civil Procedure. In any civil action arising out of a warranty obligation and relating to a matter considered in such a procedure, any decision in such procedure shall be admissible in evidence.

(4) The Commission on its own initiative may, or upon written complaint filed by any interested person shall, review the bona fide operation of any dispute settlement procedure resort to which is stated in a written warranty to be a prerequisite to pursuing a legal remedy under this section. If the Commission finds that such procedure or its implementation fails to comply with the requirements of the rules under paragraph (2), the Commission may take appropriate remedial action under any authority it may have under this chapter or any other provision of law.

(5) Until rules under paragraph (2) take effect, this subsection shall not affect the validity of any informal dispute settlement procedure respecting consumer warranties, but in any action under subsection (d) of this section, the court may invalidate any such procedure if it finds that such procedure is unfair.

(b) Prohibited acts

It shall be a violation of section 45(a)

(1) of this title for any person to fail to comply with any requirement imposed on such person by this chapter (or a rule thereunder) or to violate any prohibition contained in this chapter (or a rule thereunder).

(c) Injunction proceedings by Attorney General or Commission for deceptive warranty, noncompliance with requirements, or violating prohibitions; procedures; definitions

(1) The district courts of the United States shall have jurisdiction of any action brought by the Attorney General (in his capacity as such), or by the Commission by any of its attorneys designated by it for such purpose, to restrain—

(A) any warrantor from making a deceptive warranty with respect to a consumer product, or

(B) any person from failing to comply with any requirement imposed on such person by or pursuant to this chapter or from violating any prohibition contained in this chapter. Upon proper showing that, weighing the equities and considering the Commission's or Attorney General's likelihood of ultimate success, such action would be in the public interest and after notice to the defendant, a temporary restraining order or preliminary injunction may be granted without bond. In the case of an action brought by the Commission, if a complaint under section 45 of this title is not filed within such period (not exceeding 10 days) as may be specified by the court after the issuance of the temporary restraining order or preliminary injunction, the order or injunction shall be dissolved by the court and be of no further force and effect. Any suit shall be brought in the district in which such person resides or transacts business. Whenever it appears to the court that the ends of justice require that other persons should be parties in the action, the court may cause them to be summoned whether or not they reside in the district in which the court is held, and to that end process may be served in any district.

(2) For the purposes of this subsection, the term "deceptive warranty" means—

(A) a written warranty which—

(i) contains an affirmation, promise, description, or representation which is either false or fraudulent, or which, in light of all of the circumstances, would mislead a reasonable individual exercising due care; or

(ii) fails to contain information which is necessary in light of all of the circumstances, to make the warranty not misleading to a reasonable individual exercising due care; or

(B) a written warranty created by the use of such terms as "guaranty" or "warranty", if the terms and conditions of such warranty so limit its scope and application as to deceive a reasonable individual.

(d) Civil action by consumer for damages, etc.; jurisdiction; recovery of costs and expenses; cognizable claims

(1) Subject to subsections (a)(3) and (e) of this section, a consumer who is damaged by the failure of a supplier, warrantor, or service contractor to comply with any obligation under this chapter, or under a written warranty, implied warranty, or service contract, may bring suit for damages and other legal and equitable relief—

(A) in any court of competent jurisdiction in any State or the District of Columbia; or

(B) in an appropriate district court of the United States, subject to paragraph (3) of this subsection.

(2) If a consumer finally prevails in any action brought under paragraph (1) of this subsection, he may be allowed by the court to recover as part of the judgment a sum equal to the aggregate amount of cost and expenses (including attorneys' fees based on actual time expended) determined by the court to have been reasonably incurred by the plaintiff for or in connection with the commencement and prosecution of such action, unless the court in its discretion shall determine that such an award of attorneys' fees would be inappropriate.

(3) No claim shall be cognizable in a suit brought under paragraph (1)(B) of this subsection—

(A) if the amount in controversy of any individual claim is less than the sum or value of $25;

(B) if the amount in controversy is less than the sum or value of $50,000 (exclusive of interests and costs) computed on the basis of all claims to be determined in this suit; or

(C) if the action is brought as a class action, and the number of named plaintiffs is less than one hundred.

(e) Class actions; conditions; procedures applicable

No action (other than a class action or an action respecting a warranty to which subsection (a)(3) of this section applies) may be brought under subsection (d) of this section for failure to comply with any obligation under any written or implied warranty or service contract, and a class of consumers may not proceed in a class action under such subsection with respect to such a failure except to the extent the court determines necessary to establish the representative capacity of the named plaintiffs, unless the person obligated under the warranty or service contract is afforded a reasonable opportunity to cure such failure to comply. In the case of such a class action (other than a class action respecting a warranty to which subsection (a)(3) of this section applies) brought under subsection (d) of this section for breach of any written or implied warranty or service contract, such reasonable opportunity will be afforded by the named plaintiffs and they shall at that time notify the defendant that they are acting on behalf of the class. In the case of such a class action which is brought in a district court of the United States, the representative capacity of the named plaintiffs shall be established in the application of rule 23 of the Federal Rules of Civil Procedure.

(f) Warrantors subject to enforcement of remedies

For purposes of this section, only the warrantor actually making a written affirmation of fact, promise, or undertaking shall be deemed to have created a written warranty, and any rights arising thereunder may be enforced under this section only against such warrantor and no other person.

SEC. 2311.—APPLICABILITY TO OTHER LAWS

(a) Federal Trade Commission Act and Federal Seed Act

(1) Nothing contained in this chapter shall be construed to repeal, invalidate, or supersede the Federal Trade Commission Act (15 U.S.C. 41 et seq.) or any statute defined therein as an Antitrust Act.

(2) Nothing in this chapter shall be construed to repeal, invalidate, or supersede the Federal Seed Act (7 U.S.C. 1551 et seq.) and nothing in this chapter shall apply to seed for planting.

(b) Rights, remedies, and liabilities

(1) Nothing in this chapter shall invalidate or restrict any right or remedy of any consumer under State law or any other Federal law.

(2) Nothing in this chapter (other than sections 2308 and 2304(a)(2) and (4) of this title) shall

(A) affect the liability of, or impose liability on, any person for personal injury, or

(B) supersede any provision of State law regarding consequential damages for injury to the person or other injury.

(c) State warranty laws

(1) Except as provided in subsection (b) of this section and in paragraph (2) of this subsection, a State requirement—

(A) which relates to labeling or disclosure with respect to written warranties or performance thereof;

(B) which is within the scope of an applicable requirement of sections 2302, 2303, and 2304 of this title (and rules implementing such sections), and

(C) which is not identical to a requirement of section 2302, 2303, or 2304 of this title (or a rule thereunder), shall not be applicable to written warranties complying with such sections (or rules thereunder).

(2) If, upon application of an appropriate State agency, the Commission determines (pursuant to rules issued in accordance with

section 2309 of this title) that any requirement of such State covering any transaction to which this chapter applies—

(A) affords protection to consumers greater than the requirements of this chapter and

(B) does not unduly burden interstate commerce, then such State requirement shall be applicable (notwithstanding the provisions of paragraph (1) of this subsection) to the extent specified in such determination for so long as the State administers and enforces effectively any such greater requirement.

(d) Other Federal warranty laws

This chapter (other than section 2302(c) of this title) shall be inapplicable to any written warranty the making or content of which is otherwise governed by Federal law. If only a portion of a written warranty is so governed by Federal law, the remaining portion shall be subject to this chapter.

SEC. 2312.—EFFECTIVE DATES

(a) Effective date of chapter

Except as provided in subsection (b) of this section, this chapter shall take effect 6 months after January 4, 1975, but shall not apply to consumer products manufactured prior to such date.

(b) Effective date of section 2302(a)

Section 2302(a) of this title shall take effect 6 months after the final publication of rules respecting such section; except that the Commission, for good cause shown, may postpone the applicability of such sections until one year after such final publication in order to permit any designated classes of suppliers to bring their written warranties into compliance with rules promulgated pursuant to this chapter.

(c) Promulgation of rules

The Commission shall promulgate rules for initial implementation of this chapter as soon as possible after January 4, 1975.

Repair Log

Vehicle _____ Date Purchased _____ Mileage _____

Date In / Mileage In	Date Out / Mileage Out	Dealer Repair Shop	Repair Order Number	Service Requested Description Of Problems (Repair Order / Work Order)	Work Performed (Invoice)	Charge (if any)

Record all Repairs, including routine maintenance such as Oil Changes and Tune-Ups. While the vehicle is under Warranty, you may not be given an Invoice, when the car is picked up, because there was "no charge". Demand an Invoice (it's your right) since it details what was or was not repaired. If there are any incidental charges such as Towing, Lodging, or any other out of pocket expenses, record the charge and attach a copy of the Invoice or Sales Receipt.

Page _____

APPENDIX 13:
SAMPLE TECHNICAL SERVICE BULLETIN

Service Bulletin Mazda North American Operations
Irvine, CA 92618-2922

Subject:		Bulletin No:	04-003/02
REAR BRAKE NOISE AFTER LONG TERM STORAGE		Last Issued:	9/20/2002

APPLICABLE MODEL(S)/VINS

All 2001-2002 Miatas

DESCRIPTION

After the vehicle has been washed and not moved for a long period, a stick-slip noise may be heard from the rear brakes once the vehicle is moved. When the vehicle sits for a long period with moisture on the rear brakes, corrosion appears between the pad and disc plate. The corrosion causes the pad and disc plate to stick together. The pad and the disc plate separates when the vehicle is moved, resulting in a stick-slip noise.

Follow the information outlined below to replace the rear brake pads with new service parts.

REPAIR PROCEDURE

1. Review customer complaint.
2. Refer to PART(S) INFORMATION below to determine the correct service brake pad part number.
3. Remove and replace the rear brake pads according to appropriate Workshop Manual (Section 04).
4. Verify repair.

PART(S) INFORMATION

Part Number	Description	Qty.	Notes
N0Y0 26 48Z	Disc pad, rear	1	Disc plate dimentions: (outer diameter X thickness) 251 mm (9.98 in) X 9.0 mm (0.35 in) (Models originally-equipped with 15" tires.)
N0Y1 26 48Z	Disc pad, rear	1	Disc plate dimentions: (outer diameter X thickness) 276 mm (10.8 in) X 10.0 mm (0.39 in) (Models originally-equipped with 16" tires.)

Page 1 of 2

Bulletin No: 04-003/02	Last Issued: 9/20/2002

WARRANTY INFORMATION

Note: This information applies to verified customer complaints on vehicles covered under normal warranty. Refer to the SRT microfiche for warranty term information.

Warranty Type	A
Symptom Code	82
Damage Code	9E
Part Number Main Cause	N0Y0 26 48Z or N0Y1 26 48Z
Quantity	1
Operation Number / Labor Hours:	XX379XRX / 0.5 (L & R rear brake pads)

Page 2 of 2

APPENDIX 14:
CAR MAINTENANCE CHECKLIST

VEHICLE SYSTEM OR PART	MAINTENANCE SCHEDULE	COMMENT
Air Filter	Check every two months	Inspect and replace when dirty
Antifreeze	Check weekly	Add 50/50% solution when needed
Battery	Check with every oil change	None
Belts	Check monthly	Inspect for slack between pulleys
Brake Fluid	Check monthly	Add approved type when needed
Engine Oil	Check level every other fuel fill up	Change every three months or 3000 miles
Exhaust	Have emissions checked yearly	None
Hoses	Check monthly	Inspect for softness and bulges
Lights/Fuses	n/a	Keep spare bulbs and fuses in vehicles
Oil Filter	n/a	Replace with every oil change
Power Steering Fluid	Check monthly	Add approved type when needed
Shock Absorbers	n/a	Replace when worn or leaking
Tires	Check monthly	Inflate to recommended pressure level

VEHICLE SYSTEM OR PART	MAINTENANCE SCHEDULE	COMMENT
Transmission Fluid	Check monthly	Check with engine running and add approved type when needed
Washer Fluid	Check with every other fill up	None

MAINTENANCE TIPS

1. Check the antifreeze/coolant level weekly. Some cars have transparent reservoirs with level markings. Fill to level marking with 50/50 solution of anti-freeze and water. Caution: Do not remove the pressure cap when engine is hot.

2. Inspect belts and hoses monthly. Replace worn, glazed or frayed belts. Tighten them when more than ½" of slack can be depressed between the pulleys. Vehicles with spring loaded belt tensioners require no adjustment. Replace bulging, rotten, or brittle hoses and tighten clamps. If a hose looks bad, or feels too soft or too hard, it should be replaced.

3. Check transmission fluid monthly with engine warm and running, and parking brake on. Shift to drive, then to park. Remove dipstick, wipe dry, insert it and remove it again. Add the approved type fluid, if needed. Do not overfill!

4. Check oil every other fill up. Remove the dipstick, wipe it clean. Insert it fully and remove it again. If it is low, add oil. To maintain peak performance, change oil every 3,000 miles or 3 months, whichever comes first. Replace oil filter with every oil change.

5. Check the air filter every other month. Replace it when it's dirty or as part of a tune-up. It is easy to reach, right under the big metal "lid" in a carbureted engine; or in a rectangular box at the forward end of the air duct hose assembly, with fuel injection.

6. Check brake fluid monthly. First, wipe dirt from the brake master cylinder reservoir lid. Pry off the retainer clip and remove the lid or unscrew plastic lid, depending on which type your vehicle has. If you need fluid, add the approved type and check for possible leaks throughout the system. Fill to mark on reservoir. Caution: Do not overfill.

7. Keep windshield washer fluid reservoir full. When topping off, use some windshield washer fluid on a rag to clean off the wiper blades. In winter months, pay attention to the freezing point of the washer fluid.

8. Use extreme caution when handling a battery since it can produce explosive gases. Do not smoke, create a spark or light a match near a battery and always wear protective glasses and gloves. Have it checked with every oil change. Cables should be attached securely and be free of corrosion. If battery has filler holes, add only clear, odorless drinking water.

9. Check power steering fluid level once per month. Simply remove the reservoir dipstick. If the level is down, add fluid and inspect the pump and hoses for leaks.

10. Inspect windshield wiper blades whenever you clean your windshield. Do not wait until rubber is worn or brittle to replace them. Wiper blades should be replaced at least once per year, and more often if smearing or chattering occurs.

11. Be sure all your lights are clean and working, including brake lights, turn signals and emergency flashers. Keep spare bulbs and fuses in your vehicle.

12. Keep tires inflated to recommended pressure (it helps to own your own gauge). Check for cuts, bulges and excessive tread wear. Uneven wear indicates tires are misaligned or out of balance. Keep a record of tire rotation. Rotate at the first 5,000 miles and every 7,500 miles thereafter.

13. Look for signs of oil seepage on shock absorbers. Test shock action by bouncing the car up and down. The car should stop bouncing when you step back. Worn or leaking shocks should be replaced.

14. Look underneath for loose or broken exhaust clamps and supports. Check for holes in muffler or pipes. Replace rusted or damaged parts. Have emission checked at least once per year for compliance with local laws.

SOURCE: Federal Consumer Information Center

APPENDIX 15:
IOWA MOTOR VEHICLE DEFECT NOTIFICATION FORM

Motor Vehicle Defect Notification
(Please print clearly in ink)

Pursuant to the Iowa Lemon Law, notice is given to the manufacturer as follows:

Check All that Apply

☐ **The vehicle has been out of service at least 20 cumulative days to repair one or more malfunctions or conditions that cause the vehicle not to conform to the warranty.**

☐ **Three or more repair attempts have been made to repair the same defect or condition.**

☐ **The vehicle has been in the shop one time by reason of a defect likely to cause death or substantial bodily injury.**

Description of continuing defect(s) or condition(s) _____

_____

_____

(NOTE: this is not a complete description; the manufacturer should ascertain all appropriate information.)

I am requesting that you make a final attempt to correct the continuing substantial defect(s) or condition(s).

Vehicle Make _____ Model _____ Year _____

VIN _/_/_/_/_/_/_/_/_/_/_/_/_/_/_/_/_/

Name and City/State of selling dealer or leasing company: _____

_____

Date of Delivery _____   Odometer Reading at Delivery _____

Today's Date _____   Current Odometer Reading _____

Name and City/State of authorized service agent(s) attempting previous repairs: _____

_____

Consumer _____   Home phone _____

Address _____   Work phone _____

_____   Signature _____

_____   Date Mailed _____

APPENDIX 16:
DIRECTORY OF AUTOMOBILE DISPUTE RESOLUTION PROGRAMS

COMPANY	ADDRESS	TELEPHONE	FAX	WEBSITE	FUNCTION
Center for Auto Safety (CAS)	1825 Connecticut Ave., NW Suite 330, Washington, DC 20009	202-328-7700	n/a	www.autosafety.org	CAS advocates on behalf of consumers in auto safety and quality, fuel efficiency, emissions, and related issues. For advice on specific problems, CAS requests that consumers write a brief statement of the problem or question; include the year, make, model of the vehicle, and include a stamped self-addressed envelope.

COMPANY	ADDRESS	TELEPHONE	FAX	WEBSITE	FUNCTION
BBB AUTO LINE	Council of Better Business Bureaus Inc., 4200 Wilson Blvd., Suite 800, Arlington, VA 22203-1838	1-800-955-5100	703-525-8277	info@cbbb.bbb.org www.bbb.org	Third-party dispute resolution program for automobile manufacturers.
Office of Defects Investigation	DOT Auto Safety Hotline, 400 7th Street SW, Washington, DC 20590	1-800-424-9153	202-366-7882	www.nhtsa.dot.gov/hotline	Consumers can contact the DOT Auto Safety Hotline to report safety defects in vehicles, tires, and child safety seats. Information is available about air bags, child safety seats, seat belts, and general highway safety. Consumers who experience a safety defect in their vehicle are encouraged to report the defect to the Hotline in addition to the dealer or manufacturer.

COMPANY	ADDRESS	TELEPHONE	FAX	WEBSITE	FUNCTION
Motorist Assurance Program	7101 Wisconsin Ave., Suite 1200, Bethesda MD 20814	301-634-4954	202-318-0378	www.motorist.org	MAP accredits those auto repair shops that apply and follow industry developed standards for inspecting vehicles as well as meet other requirements, handles inquiries/disputes between accredited shops and customers and offers information to consumers about how to locate a repair shop how to talk to a technician and how to gain satisfaction from auto repair shops.
National Automobile Dealers Association	8400 Westpark Dr., McLean VA 22102	1-800-252-6232	703-821-7075	www.nada.org	Third-party dispute resolution program administered through the National Automobile Dealers Association. Consumer information available on request.

COMPANY	ADDRESS	TELEPHONE	FAX	WEBSITE	FUNCTION
National Institute for Automotive Service Excellence (ASE)	101 Blue Seal Dr. SE, Suite 101, Leesburg, VA 20175	703-669-6600	n/a	www.asecert.org	ASE is an independent, national nonprofit organization founded in 1972 to help improve the quality of automotive service and repair through the voluntary testing and certification of automotive repair professionals. More than 424,000 ASE-certified technicians work in dealerships, independent repair shops, service stations, auto parts stores, fleets and schools. ASE publishes several consumer publications about auto maintenance and repair.

Source: Federal Citizen Information Center, U.S. General Services Administration.

APPENDIX 17:
SAMPLE REQUEST FOR ARBITRATION UNDER THE NEW YORK LEMON LAW ARBITRATION PROGRAM

INSTRUCTIONS FOR COMPLETING
THE NEW CAR LEMON LAW
REQUEST FOR ARBITRATION FORM

To participate in the New York State New Car Lemon Law Arbitration Program, you must complete the attached form. Be as accurate and complete as possible. Please attach **copies** of all relevant documents (including your purchase or lease agreement, all service or work orders relating to the problem for which you seek this arbitration, and any correspondence between you and the manufacturer or its authorized dealer relating to such problem). **DO NOT SEND ORIGINAL DOCUMENTS.** Sign and return the completed form, together with your documents, to:

New York State Attorney General's Office
120 Broadway --3rd floor
New York, NY 10271
Attention: NEW CAR LEMON LAW ARBITRATION UNIT.

The Attorney General's Office will review your form and advise you whether your claim is accepted in the arbitration program. If the form is accepted, you will be notified by the Attorney General's Office which will then forward your form and documents to the **New York State Dispute Resolution Association (NYSDRA)**, the Program Administrator. NYSDRA will then notify you to send it the required $250 filing fee. Upon receipt of the filing fee, NYSDRA will begin processing your claim. If your form is rejected by the Attorney General's Office, it will be returned to you with a statement indicating the reason for its rejection.

DO NOT SEND FILING FEE UNTIL YOU ARE REQUESTED TO BY NYSDRA.

Please remember to sign and date the form. **Failure to complete any question or submit documents may result in a rejection of the form.**

NOTICE:
THE ARBITRATOR'S DECISION UNDER THIS PROGRAM IS BINDING ON BOTH PARTIES, SUBJECT TO A LIMITED RIGHT OF APPEAL TO COURT BY EITHER PARTY. YOU MAY WISH TO CONSULT AN ATTORNEY BEFORE PARTICIPATING IN THIS PROGRAM. PLEASE READ "NEW YORK'S NEW CAR LEMON LAW: A GUIDE FOR CONSUMERS" CAREFULLY BEFORE COMPLETING THIS FORM.

Case No. _____

                    Referred To NYSDRA _____

                    Filing Date   _____

NEW YORK STATE ATTORNEY GENERAL'S OFFICE
ELIOT SPITZER, ATTORNEY GENERAL

NEW YORK NEW CAR LEMON LAW ARBITRATION PROGRAM
REQUEST FOR ARBITRATION FORM

CONSUMER INFORMATION

1.   Name: _____

      Address: _____

      City: _____   State:_____Zip:_____

      Phone: Home (_____)_____-_____   Work:(_____)_____-_____

VEHICLE INFORMATION (Attach Copy of Your Bill of Sale or Lease)

2.   Manufacturer: _____
            (GM, Ford, Chrysler, Toyota, Winnebago, etc.)

3.   Year: _____   Make: _____   Model: _____
                  (ex. Chevrolet, Dodge)   (ex. Cavalier, Caravan)

4.   Vehicle Identification Number (VIN):_____

5.   Date of delivery?_____ Mileage at delivery:_____ Current Mileage: _____

6.   Did you purchase or lease your vehicle in New York? .... Yes[ ] No[ ]
      [ ] I purchased my vehicle.   [ ]   I leased my vehicle.

7.   Is your vehicle registered in New York?...................................... Yes[ ] No[ ]

8.   Is your vehicle primarily used for personal, family or
      household purposes? .... Yes[ ] No[ ]

9.   Do you still own or lease your vehicle? .... Yes[ ] No[ ]

1

DEALER INFORMATION

10.   Name: _____

        Address: _____

        City: _____ State:_____ Zip:_____

BANK OR FINANCING INSTITUTION (if financed):

11.   Name: _____

        Address: _____

        City: _____ State:_____ Zip:_____

LEASING COMPANY (if leased):

12.   Name: _____

        Address: _____

        City: _____ State:_____ Zip: _____

        Lease Acct #: _____

VEHICLE'S PROBLEM(S)

13.   Briefly describe the problem(s) for which you seek a refund or a replacement vehicle:

        _____

        _____

14.   Does the problem(s) for which you seek relief substantially impair the
value of the vehicle to you? .... Yes [ ] No [ ]

15.   On what date and at what mileage did you **first** report this problem(s)
to the dealer or the manufacturer?   Date: _____ Mileage: _____

16.   Does the problem(s) involve a dealer installed option? .... Yes [ ] No [ ]
        Specify: _____

2

BASIS FOR RELIEF SOUGHT: You must complete at least one of the following three questions (17, 18 or 19). If you have a Motor Home, you must also answer # 20.

17. **Unsuccessful Repair Attempts**

   A. How many repair attempts for the **same** problem were made within the first 18,000 miles or 24 months, whichever is earlier? _____

   B. Give the date, mileage and work order number for each of the repair attempts by an authorized dealer for the **same** problem.

   Problem 1 (Specify) _____

	Date	Mileage	Work Order #
(1)			
(2)			
(3)			
(4)			

   Problem 2 (Specify) _____

	Date	Mileage	Work Order #
(1)			
(2)			
(3)			
(4)			

   C. Do you have copies of all relevant work orders?................... Yes [ ] No [ ]
   (If yes, attach copies of them. Otherwise, once accepted into the Program, you may request copies from the manufacturer, with the arbitrator's approval, by writing to the Administrator pursuant to Regulation §300.9.)

   D. Did the problem continue to exist at the end of the fourth attempt? Yes [ ] No [ ]

3

18. **Days in Shop for Repairs**

   A.   How many days was the vehicle out of service due to repairs within the first 18,000 miles
        or 24 months, whichever is earlier?   _____ days.

   B.   List the dates, mileage, and repair order numbers for those repairs:

   From:_____ To:_____   Days out:_____ Mileage:_____   Work Order #_____

   From:_____ To:_____   Days out:_____ Mileage:_____   Work Order #_____

   From:_____ To:_____   Days out:_____ Mileage:_____   Work Order #_____

   From:_____ To:_____   Days out:_____ Mileage:_____   Work Order #_____

   C.   Do you have copies of all relevant work orders?..............   Yes [ ] No [ ]
        (If yes, attach copies of them. Otherwise, once accepted into the Program, you may
        request copies from the manufacturer, with the arbitrator's approval, by writing to the
        Administrator pursuant to Regulation §300.9.)

19. **Refusal to Repair (Note: This question should only be completed if the dealer and the
    manufacturer refuse to commence repairs.)**

   A.   Did you first notify the **dealer** of the problem for which you are
        seeking this arbitration? ....   Yes [ ] No [ ]

   B.   If yes, what problem(s)? _____

   C.   What was the date of notification to the dealer?   _____

   D.   Did the dealer refuse to inspect the vehicle and make whatever repairs were necessary
        within 7 days of receiving your initial notice of the problem?..   Yes [ ] No [ ]

   E.   If yes, did you notify the **manufacturer** by certified mail, return receipt requested, of
        such refusal? (Attach copy of notification with proof of mailing.) Yes [ ] No [ ]

   F.   Did the manufacturer fail to make repairs within 20 days of receiving
        your written notice of the dealer's refusal to repair?............   Yes [ ] No [ ]

4

20. **If Your Complaint Involves a Motor Home:**

A. Did the dealer or manufacturer provide you with a written copy of the special lemon law notification requirements? .... Yes [ ] No [ ]

B. If the answer to (A) is yes, prior to this application for arbitration, did you notify the dealer or the manufacturer, by certified mail, return receipt requested, of a defect or condition that was subject to repair at least **2** times, or that the motor home has been out of service by reason of repair for **21** days, whichever occurs first? (If yes, attach copy of the notification with proof of mailing.) .... Yes [ ] No [ ]

C. If the answer to both (A) and (B) is yes, was the motor home out of service for a total of at least 30 days (the last 9 days **after** the notice is given to the manufacturer), or was the motor home in the shop for repairs 3 or more times (the 3rd repair attempt **after** the notice is given to the manufacturer) for the same problem?........ Yes [ ] No [ ]

HEARING LOCATION

21. Please indicate where you want the arbitration hearing to be held:

[ ] Albany	[ ] Hempstead	[ ] Oneida
[ ] Amsterdam	[ ] Highland	[ ] Oneonta
[ ] Auburn	[ ] Hudson	[ ] Oswego
[ ] Batavia	[ ] Ilion	[ ] Penn Yan
[ ] Binghamton	[ ] Ithaca	[ ] Plattsburgh
[ ] Bronx	[ ] Jamaica	[ ] Poughkeepsie
[ ] Brooklyn	[ ] Jamestown	[ ] Rochester
[ ] Buffalo	[ ] Johnstown	[ ] Saratoga Springs
[ ] Canandaigua	[ ] Lake Placid	[ ] Schenectady
[ ] Carmel	[ ] Lower Manhattan	[ ] Smithtown
[ ] Catskill	[ ] Lowville	[ ] Speculator
[ ] Cobleskill	[ ] Lyons	[ ] Staten Island
[ ] Corning	[ ] Malone	[ ] Syracuse
[ ] Cortland	[ ] Monticello	[ ] Troy
[ ] Delhi	[ ] Montour Falls	[ ] Upper Manhattan
[ ] Elmira	[ ] New City	[ ] Utica
[ ] Fort Edward	[ ] Niagara Falls	[ ] Waterloo
[ ] Geneseo	[ ] Norwich	[ ] Watertown
[ ] Glens Falls	[ ] Ogdensburg	[ ] Yonkers
[ ] Goshen	[ ] Olean	

5

TYPE OF HEARING AND RELIEF REQUESTED

22.   [ ] Oral (in person)   [ ] Documents only (if manufacturer agrees)

23.   If successful, I wish to receive a:
      [ ] full refund   [ ] comparable replacement vehicle

PREVIOUS ARBITRATION

24.   A.   Did you participate in any previous arbitration for the
           same problem(s) for which you now seek arbitration?......   Yes [ ]   No [ ]

      B.   If yes, what was the name of the Program? _____

      C.   Did you accept the decision of the arbitrator? ....   Yes [ ]   No [ ]

      D.   Did the manufacturer comply with the decision?.............   Yes [ ]   No [ ]

      E.   Date of Decision: _____ (attach copy of decision)

SIGNATURE: _____Date: _____

CNS 006 (5/05)

6

GLOSSARY

Accident—An unforeseen event, occurring without intent or design on the part of the person whose act caused it.

Accord and Satisfaction—Accord and satisfaction refers to the payment of money, or other thing of value, which is usually less than the amount owed or demanded, in exchange for extinguishment of the debt.

Airbag Deployment —Occurs when the driver, passenger or side airbag has been used or deployed during a crash or other incident. If an airbag has been deployed, new or recycled airbags must be installed for the airbag system to return to operation.

American Arbitration Association (AAA)—National organization of arbitrators from whose panel arbitrators are selected for labor and civil disputes.

Arbitration—The reference of a dispute to an impartial person chosen by the parties to the dispute who agree in advance to abide by the arbitrator's award issued after a hearing at which both parties have an opportunity to be heard.

As Is—Refers to the sale of an item for which the gives no warranties to the buyer and the buyer purchases the item and assumes the risk of its condition

Automotive Recycler —Automotive Recyclers often sell vehicles classified as "totaled" by insurance companies. The majority of these vehicles are rebuilt and sold as a complete vehicle, dismantled and sold for parts, or scrapped and sold as metal. On occasion, they also handle vehicles with no specific damage history.

Award—The final and binding decision of an arbitrator, made in writing and enforceable in court under state and federal statutes.

Bill—As referred to in commercial law, an account for goods sold, services rendered and work done.

Bill of Sale—A written agreement by which the exchange of personal property is made.

Breach of Warranty—An infraction of an express or implied agreement as to the title, quality, content or condition of a thing which is sold.

Built to Non U.S. Standards—Vehicle previously registered or titled outside of the U.S. and may not comply with U.S. safety and emissions standards.

Caveat Emptor—Latin for "let the buyer beware." A rule of law that the purchaser buys at his or her own risk.

Caveat Venditor—Latin for "Let the seller beware."

Certified Pre-Owned Vehicle—Many manufacturers have certified pre-owned programs that promote used vehicles that meet high standards defined by the manufacturer. Each program has a different certification process.

Collision Repair Facility—A collision repair facility specializes in repairing vehicle damage caused by accidents and other incidents. A vehicle inspection completed by your dealer or a professional inspector is recommended.

Commercial Vehicle—Vehicle registered for business purposes.

Compensatory Damages—Those damages directly referable to the tortious act, and which can be readily proven, for which the injured party should be compensated as a matter of right.

Consumer—A buyer of any consumer product.

Consumer Expectation—The expectation of a reasonable consumer as to the safety characteristics, limitations or condition of a product.

Consumer Product—Any product which is distributed in commerce and which is normally used for personal, family, or household purposes.

Contract—A contract is an agreement between two or more persons which creates an obligation to do or not to do a particular thing

Curbstoning—A curbstoner is a person who purchases vehicles at volumes that require a dealer license and then poses as a private seller to sell to unsuspecting buyers for a large profit. Curbstoning is illegal in most States

Damages—In general, damages refers to monetary compensation which the law awards to one who has been injured by the actions of another, such as in the case of tortious conduct or breach of contractual obligations.

Damage Disclosure—When the owner discloses to a DMV that the vehicle sustained damage. The extent of damage can range from minor to severe.

Defective—Lacking an essential; incomplete, deficient, faulty.

Disclaimer—Words or conduct which tend to negate or limit warranty in the sale of goods, which in certain instances must be conspicuous and refer to the specific warranty to be excluded.

Disclosure—Disclosure is the act of disclosing or revealing that which is secret or not fully understood.

Dismantled Title—The vehicle sustained major damage to one or more major component parts and the cost of repairing the vehicle for safe operation exceeds its fair market value. When a Dismantled title is issued, the vehicle may be used only for parts or scrap metal. It cannot be re-titled or returned to the road.

Down Payment—A partial payment of the purchase price.

Duty—The obligation, to which the law will give recognition and effect, to conform to a particular standard of conduct toward another.

Exceeds Mechanical Limits—A vehicle with a 5-digit odometer cannot accurately track mileage after 99,999 miles because the odometer rolls over. This title is the result of a seller certifying under the Truth-in-Mileage Act, that the odometer reading "exceeds mechanical limits" of the odometer.

Exempt Vehicle—In most states, odometer law requires that vehicles less than 10 years old report odometer readings. Vehicles over 10 years old are often exempt from this requirement and do not need to provide odometer readings.

Express Warranty—A promise relating to the quality or condition of property which is usually reduced to writing.

Failed Emissions Inspection—The emissions check performed during a vehicle inspection indicated the vehicle was emitting more than allowable emissions standards and/or had missing or modified parts.

Federal Trade Commission—The Federal Trade Commission is an agency of the federal government created in 1914 for the purpose of promoting free and fair competition in interstate commerce through the prevention of general trade restraints.

Finance Charge—Any charge for an extension of credit, such as interest.

First Owner—When the first owner(s) obtains a title from a Department of Motor Vehicles as proof of ownership.

Fitness—Suitable for the need or use.

Frame Damage—In most cases, a vehicle is inspected for frame damage after an accident or other incident. All levels of accidents from minor to severe can cause frame damage and in most cases it can be repaired.

Full Covenant and Warranty Deed—A deed conveying real property which contains a covenant that warrants title by each previous holder of warranty deeds.

Grey Market Vehicle—Vehicle previously registered or titled outside of the U.S. and may not comply with U.S. safety and emissions standards.

Gross Polluter —A Gross Polluter is a vehicle that fails an emissions inspection with below-standard scores. These vehicles can pollute as much as 18 times more than a vehicle that passes an emissions inspection. It is illegal to drive or sell a gross polluting vehicle in California, and it cannot be registered with the DMV.

Hazard—A condition which presents a potential for injury.

Implied Warranty—A warranty relating to the quality or condition of property that is implied by law to exist.

Inspections—Many states or counties require annual or biennial emissions and/or safety inspections. Odometer readings are collected at the time of the inspection.

Interest—An amount of money paid by a borrower to a lender for the use of the lender's money.

Judgment—A judgment is a final determination by a court of law concerning the rights of the parties to a lawsuit.

Judgment Creditor—A creditor who has obtained a judgment against a debtor, which judgment may be enforced to obtain payment of the amount due.

Judgment Debtor—An individual who owes a sum of money, and against whom a judgment has been awarded for that debt.

Junk Title—A Junk Title is issued on a vehicle damaged to the extent that the cost of repairing the vehicle for safe operation exceeds its fair market value; or a vehicle that has been declared a Total Loss by an insurer or other state or jurisdiction. Some states treat Junk titles the same as Salvage but the majority use this title to indicate that a vehicle is not road worthy and cannot be titled.

Label—Information affixed to and/or presented with a product.

Latent Defect—A hidden defect in a product that is not ordinarily discoverable upon reasonable inspection.

Lease—When someone leases a car from a dealer, the dealer actually sells the vehicle to a leasing company. The leasing company then collects payments for the vehicle from the new owner for 24, 36, 48 or more months. A leasing company can be an independent car dealer or a car manufacturer.

Lemon Law—Refers to state legislation affording certain remedies to the purchasers of new or used vehicles which are discovered to have recurrent repair problems which are not able to be resolved by the manufacturer or dealer of the vehicle.

Lemon Law Vehicle—A vehicle with major problems that has been repurchased by or had its price renegotiated with the manufacturer. The state marks its official records or issues a title brand for lemon law vehicles. Laws vary by state as to the specific requirements for a "lemon". Most manufacturers issue some buybacks that are not the result of Lemon Laws but rather a courtesy.

Lien—A lien is an ownership right to a piece of property. When a financial institution loans money to someone purchasing a vehicle, the financial institution has a lien on the vehicle. Other types of liens include mechanic's liens and child support liens.

Loan—A loan is made when a person borrows money from a financial institution or other type of lender with an agreement to pay back the full amount plus interest over a period of time. Loans are usually guaranteed with assets like a vehicle or home. Until the loan is paid off, the lender will have a lien on these assets and has the right to repossess them if the terms of the loan are not met.

Loan Principal—The loan principal is the amount of the debt not including interest or any other additions.

Magnuson-Moss Act—A federal law governing the placement and content of written warranties on consumer products.

Manufacturer Buyback—A vehicle with major problems that has been repurchased by or had its price renegotiated with the manufacturer. The state marks its official records or issues a title brand for manufacturer buyback vehicles, also known as Lemon Law vehicles. Laws vary by state as to the specific requirements for a "lemon". Most manufacturers issue some buybacks that are not the result of Lemon Laws but rather a courtesy. These buybacks are not recorded on the title.

Manufacturer Recall—Automobile manufacturers issue recall notices to inform owners of car defects that have come to the manufacturer's attention. Recalls also suggest improvements that can be made to improve the safety of a particular vehicle. Most manufacturer recalls can be repaired at no cost to the consumer.

Manufacturer-Recommended Maintenance Schedules—Automobile manufacturers provide recommended maintenance schedules for each of their models. These schedules inform owners of maintenance that should be performed on a vehicle at specific mileage milestones.

Manufacturer Vehicle—Manufacturer vehicles are vehicles put up for sale by the manufacturer. These vehicles are typically only available to dealers at special auctions. These vehicles have generally been registered as lease or rental vehicles.

Manufacturing Defect—An unintended aspect of a finished product, due to error or omission in assembly or manufacture, that causes an injury.

Misrepresentation—The legal doctrine allocating liability to a defendant that misled users or made false statements concerning the performance or safety of a product.

Misuse—The use of a product contrary to its label directions, instructions, or expected usage.

Motor Vehicle Department—Motor Vehicle Departments issue both titles and registrations to vehicle owners. New titles and registrations can be created for name, address and lien holder changes; ownership changes; vehicle status changes; registration activity; title corrections; and lost titles.

New Owner Reported—When a vehicle is sold to a new owner, the Title must be transferred to the new owner(s) at a Department of Motor Vehicles.

Not Actual Mileage Title—When the seller certifies, under the Truth-in-Mileage Act, that the odometer reading does not reflect the vehicle's actual mileage. This may occur because the odometer was tampered with, broken, or replaced.

Odometer Rollback—If a more recent odometer reading is less than an older reading, then the odometer may have been tampered with and "rolled back." The odometer readings triggering Potential Odometer Rollbacks are collected by a DMV or other verified source.

Oral Agreement—An oral agreement is one which is not in writing or not signed by the parties.

Parol Evidence Rule—The parol evidence rule is the doctrine which holds that the written terms of an agreement may not be varied by prior or oral agreements.

Patent Defect—A plainly visible defect or one that can be discovered by inspection exercising ordinary care.

Personal Use—Vehicle was registered by the owner for private or personal use.

Prima Facie Case—A case which is sufficient on its face, being supported by at least the requisite minimum of evidence, and being free from palpable defects.

Product Liability—The legal liability of manufacturers and sellers to compensate buyers, users, and even bystanders, for damages or injuries suffered because of defects in goods purchased.

Proximate Cause—That which, in a natural and continuous sequence, unbroken by any efficient intervening cause, produces injury, and without which the result would not have occurred.

Punitive Damages—Compensation in excess of compensatory damages which serve as a form of punishment to the wrongdoer who has exhibited malicious and willful misconduct.

Purchase Order—A purchase order is a document which authorizes a seller to deliver goods and is considered an offer which is accepted upon delivery.

Rebuilt/Reconstructed Vehicle—A Rebuilt/Reconstructed vehicle is a salvage vehicle that has been repaired and restored to operation. These vehicles are often severely damaged before they are rebuilt and refurbished parts are typically used during reconstruction. In most states, an inspection of the vehicle is required before the vehicle is allowed to return to the road.

Recall—The withdrawal of a marketed product from sale.

Relocation—When a vehicle is moved from one state to another with no change of ownership.

Rental—Vehicle was registered by a car rental agency.

Repossession—When a repossession occurs a vehicle owner fails to make loan payments, and the financial institution holding the title takes possession of the vehicle.

Restatement of the Law—A series of volumes authored by the American Law Institute that tell what the law in a general area is, how it is changing, and what direction the authors think this change should take, for example, the Restatement of the Law of Torts or Contracts.

Risk—Exposure to injury or loss.

Sale—An agreement to transfer property from the seller to the buyer for a stated sum of money.

Salvage Auction Record—Most vehicles sold at Salvage auctions were declared totaled by insurance companies. Most of these vehicles have sustained significant damage but there are some exceptions. For instance, recovered stolen vehicles are often declared a total loss regardless of the actual damage. Rebuilders and Recyclers purchase these vehicles at auction with intentions to rebuild them or dismantle them for parts.

Salvage Title—A Salvage Title is issued on a vehicle damaged to the extent that the cost of repairing the vehicle for safe operation exceeds its fair market value; or a vehicle that has been declared a Total Loss by an insurer or other state or jurisdiction. Some states treat Junk titles the same as Salvage but the majority use this title to indicate that a vehicle is not road worthy and cannot be titled again in that state. The following ten States also use Salvage titles to identify stolen vehicles—AZ, FL, GA, IL, MN, NJ, NM, NY, OK and OR.

Service Plan Company—Service Plan Companies market extended warranty plans to buyers of both new and used cars as mechanical breakdown insurance. Information is collected from service plan companies when they issue contracts and when they pay repair claims.

Tax—A sum of money assessed upon one's income, property and purchases, for the purpose of supporting the government.

Title Issued—A state issues a title to provide a vehicle owner with proof of ownership. Each title has a unique number.

Total Loss—An insurance company declares a vehicle a total loss when a claim exceeds the full value of the vehicle. Insurance companies typically take possession and obtain the title of such vehicles.

Truth-in-Mileage Act—The Truth in Mileage Act (TIMA) of 1986 requires a seller to disclose the vehicle's mileage on the title when ownership is transferred. Congress enacted this Act to prohibit odometer tampering and to protect consumers from mileage fraud. Under this act, sellers must disclose any issues with the vehicle's odometer.

Uniform Commercial Code (UCC)—The UCC is a code of laws governing commercial transactions which was designed to bring uniformity to the laws of the various states.

Vehicle Identification Number (VIN)—This 17 character number is unique to each vehicle. It identifies characteristics of the vehicle, including manufacturer, year, model, body, engine specifications, and serial number.

Verified Odometer Rollback—When an odometer rollback is reported to and verified by a state or province law enforcement agency.

Waiver— Intentional and voluntary surrender of some known right.

Warranty—An assurance by one party to a contract that a certain fact exists and may be relied upon by the other party to the contract.

BIBLIOGRAPHY AND
ADDITIONAL RESOURCES

Black's Law Dictionary, Fifth Edition. St. Paul, MN: West Publishing Company, 1979.

Call For Action (Date Visited: October 2005) <http://www.callfor action.org/>.

Carfax (Date Visited: October 2005) <http://www.carfax.com/>.

Consumer Affairs.com (Date Visited: October 2005) <http://www.consumeraffairs.com/lemon.law/>.

Consumer Sentinel (Date Visited: October 2005) <http://www.consumer.gov/sentinel/>.

The Federal Citizen Information Center (Date Visited: October 2005) <http://www.pueblo.gsa.gov/>.

The Federal Trade Commission (Date Visited: October 2005) <http://www.ftc/gov/>.

The International Association of Lemon Law Administrators (IALLA) (Date Visited: October 2005) <http://www.ialla.net/>.

National Highway and Traffic Safety Administration (Date Visited: October 2005) <http://www.nhtsa.dot.gov/>.

National Institute of Standards and Technology (Date Visited: October 2005) <http://www.nist.gov/>.

National Safety Council (Date Visited: October 2005) <http://www.nsc.org/>.

United States Consumer Product Safety Commission (Date Visited: October 2005) <http://www.cpsc.gov/>.